Making the Connection
Data-Informed Practices
in Academic Support Centers
for College Athletes

Making the Connection

Data-Informed Practices
in Academic Support Centers
for College Athletes

edited by

Eddie Comeaux
University of California, Riverside

INFORMATION AGE PUBLISHING, INC.
Charlotte, NC • www.infoagepub.com

Library of Congress Cataloging-in-Publication Data

A CIP record for this book is available from the Library of Congress
http://www.loc.gov

ISBN: 978-1-68123-024-5 (Paperback)
            978-1-68123-025-2 (Hardcover)
            978-1-68123-026-9 (ebook)

Printed in the United States of America

CONTENTS

FOREWORD

Estela Mara Bensimon

It is said that what is measured is what gets noticed. When it comes to athletics, the things that are measured routinely are eligibility criteria, games won and lost, other indicators of athletic performance, and the likelihood of victory over rivals. On the other hand, as *Making the Connection* makes clear, institutions of higher education appear less attentive to using data to assess the excellence of the academic performance of athletes, whose very hard work benefit the institutions they represent on the field.

This book is a call for increased vigilance over the academic performance of college athletes. Institutions need to make sure that the student athlete who is cheered in the stadium, glorified in national television, and prominently displayed in institutional materials is also earning academic credits toward on-time graduation, participating in career-enhancing internships, and receiving academic support from faculty and others. It is imperative to use data to monitor the collegiate experience of athletes because of the high concentration of Black male athletes in revenue-generating sports compared to their overall undergraduate representation. For example, at UCLA Black males account for 1.1% of undergraduates but 48.8% of basketball and football teams; And at my own university, the comparable figures are 2.2% and 56.2%. Graduation rates show tremendous gaps: at both UCLA and USC there is a −44 percentage point difference in the rates of graduation for Black male athletes and all undergraduates (Harper, Williams, Blackman, 2013). These data are emblematic of the outcomes of

Black male athletes throughout NCAA Division I colleges and universities. As Shaun Harper (2006) has observed, "Perhaps nowhere in higher education is the disenfranchisement of Black male students more insidious than in college athletics" (p. 6).

To create a comprehensive picture of the academic status of athletes, institutions need to collect and report snapshot, trend, and longitudinal data for each gender and racial/ethnic group. This data should be available to answer the following questions:

1. What is the racial or ethnic composition of men and women's athletic teams?
2. What teams have the highest concentration of students from under-represented groups?
3. What is the distribution of athletes by race, ethnicity and gender in the fields of study offered by the institution? Are students from under-represented groups concentrated in particular fields? Are they missing in other fields?
4. How many credits are completed by athletes by race, ethnicity, and gender semester by semester?
5. What is the distribution of GPA's by race, ethnicity, and gender? Are there grade or course withdrawal patterns that indicate particularly troublesome courses for athletes? Based on grade and withdrawal patterns are there high risk majors for athletes?
6. What are athletes' rates of participation in unique academic-enhancing experiences such as internships, faculty research, study abroad, and honors program?
7. For athletes at four-year colleges, what are their four- and six-year graduation rates by race, ethnicity, and gender? How do athletes' graduation rates compare to the non-athlete population by race, ethnicity, and gender?
8. For athletes in community colleges, what are their rates for earning a terminal degree or certificate? What are their rates of transfer to a four-year college? What are their rates of earning a bachelor's degree?
9. What is the amount of institutional aid provided to athletes? What is the indebtedness of athletes?
10. What is the proportion of athletes who go on to graduate school?

All institutions have the data to answer these 10 questions. However, not all institutions produce these data routinely or in a format that is conducive to analysis that enables practitioners (provost, coach, instructor, counselor) to make substantive changes in practices, structures, policies, or resource allocations. In the aptly titled report "Data Don't Drive," Alicia Dowd (2005) reminds us that too often institutions, "report data that are never actually used to guide decisions at the institutional level" (p. 1). The chapters in *Making the Connection* provide guidance on various kinds of data and how to use them for the benefit of college athletes.

In addition to institutions not collecting data on college athletes by race, ethnicity, and gender routinely as a standard operating procedure, or who collecting such data but failing to use it as a source of knowledge (for example to understand why there are racial disparities in the educational outcomes of athletes), there is the problem with making sense of data.

Sadly, I and my colleagues at the Center for Urban Education (CUE) have found that data showing big gaps in educational outcomes (for example between Whites and African Americans, or Asians and Latinos), much too often elicits responses that shift the attention away from institutional responsibility for the production of inequities. There is a strong predisposition among faculty and others to attribute differences in educational outcomes to racial and ethnic stereotypes (e.g., "their culture does not value education"), negative perceptions about motivation and aspirations, (e.g., "we have lots of resources, but they don't use them"), and rationales that despite sounding sympathetic are harmful in that they absolve practitioners (e.g., "they went to bad schools so they are not prepared" or "they lack basic study skills"). Notably, we have also found that data, particularly about African Americans, also elicits assumptions about athletics. For example, in predominantly White institutions that experience a surge of African American students, a typical reaction is, "they are probably athletes" or "they primarily come here for sports." Data that show African Americans are not doing well, are explained away as, "they are probably athletes" or "they only come to play, they don't expect to graduate."

The interpretations above are not manufactured. They have been voiced among practitioners in Equity Scorecard (http://cue.usc.edu/) teams at all types of institutions of higher education about White, Black, Latino, or Asian students. The meaning that data are given can be harmful and exacerbate educational inequalities. However, the individuals engaged in this kind of interpretation do not intend to commit harm. They have been socialized to expect that college is for individuals who know how to be college students, and when some students do not conform to the expectations of what a college student should be, then interpretations are made that impede reflection on institutional structures and policies (Bensimon, 2007). This book addresses the problem of harmful interpretations on practical strategies to support organizational learning that is reflective and oriented toward change.

To summarize, *Making the Connection* addresses the three problems I have highlighted in relation to data use:

1. Not reporting data by race, ethnicity, and gender on the educational outcomes of athletes as a routine practice.
2. Not having the structures that enable practitioners to engage in data analysis that helps them learn what changes need to be made in their practices.
3. Not safeguarding against harmful interpretations that reinforce racial deficit oriented stereotypes.

REFERENCES

Bensimon, E. M. (2007). The underestimated significance of practitioner knowledge in the scholarship of student success. *Review of Higher Education, 30,* 441–469.

Dowd, A. C. (2005, December). *Data don't drive: Building a practitioner-driven culture of inquiry to assess community college performance.* Indianapolis, IN: Lumina Foundation for Education.

Harper, S. R. (2006). *Black male students at public universities in the U.S.: Status, trends and implications for policy and practice.* Washington, DC: Joint Center for Political and Economic Studies.

Harper, S. R., Williams, C. D., & Blackman, H. W. (2013). *Black male student-athletes and racial inequities in NCAA Division I college sports.* Philadelphia, PA: University of Pennsylvania, Center for the Study of Race and Equity in Education.

Estela Mara Bensimon, EdD, is a professor of higher education and codirector of the Center for Urban Education (CUE) at the USC Rossier School of Education. Her current research is on issues of racial equity in higher education from the perspective of organizational learning and socio-cultural practice theories. She is particularly interested in place-based, practitioner-driven inquiry as a means of organizational change in higher education.

PREFACE

Eddie Comeaux

Over the past several decades, college athletes have shifted even more prominently into the spotlight, yet scholarly discussions related to the chasm between research and practice in the academic support centers designed to support them, have been conspicuously absent. Because of this disconnect, higher education practitioners appear to be out of sync with athletes' needs and are negligent of the positive benefits of data-driven practices. Consequently, there is a growing urgency to initiate discussions between researchers and salient stakeholders in the affairs of intercollegiate athletics, and to offer cutting-edge ideas that attempt to close this critical gap.

The National Collegiate Athletic Association (NCAA)'s recent legislation on the academic progress rate (APR) underscores this divide between research and practice in support centers for athletes. Under the APR metric, which attempts to enhance the academic performance of athletes in Division 1 team sports, each athlete earns a maximum of two points: one for maintaining academic eligibility and another for staying in school. Team members' scores are tallied and divided by the total number of possible points, and then multiplied by 1,000, yielding a maximum score of 1,000. Teams that fall short of the 930 APR threshold are subjected to contemporaneous penalties, such as scholarship reductions and a ban from post-season competition. According to the NCAA, 35 teams faced APR penalties during the 2012–2013 season.

Making the Connection, pages xi–xiv
Copyright © 2015 by Information Age Publishing

In part because of these unfavorable results, the APR initiative has begun to pressure higher education practitioners to rethink their current practices. Reformers of college athletics have recommended that, as a starting point, NCAA member institutions—and practitioners in particular—identify strengths and problem areas that impact team members' academic performance. This approach requires practitioners to utilize baseline data to understand how athletes participate in the athletic, social, and academic systems of college. In short, they must demonstrate that their educational practices are supported by empirical evidence. They must not only understand what data-driven practices look like, but also become skilled in using evidence for planning, decision-making, evaluation, and accountability. There is, however, a severe lack of data-driven approaches that inform decision making in this context. Comeaux (2012), for example, discovered that fewer than 3% of advisors and counselors in academic support centers for athletes at Division 1 colleges and universities provide programs and services that include assessment plans to measure the impact of their work on learning outcomes. Instead, practitioners generally rely on and engage in practices that are largely based on intuition.

Data-driven practices, coupled with assessment tools to understand if and how program outcomes are being achieved, are imperative. Without these components, it becomes almost impossible to offer feedback, to identify strengths or critical problem areas, or to reveal performance gaps that must be addressed in order to increase the academic productivity of college athletes. In this context, a growing number of aspiring practitioners are enrolling in graduate programs in athletics administration, higher education student affairs, sports management, sports studies, and sports leadership.

Quite frequently, graduate programs in these fields offer relevant courses on leadership and intercollegiate athletics, or some variation thereof, for example: leadership, theory, and practice in intercollegiate athletics; introduction to athletic administration; and intercollegiate athletics and the college student athlete. Yet no supplementary sources exist on data-driven best practices in intercollegiate athletics. Such insights are critical for forging deeper and creating more authentically responsive intervention strategies for athletes. In the absence of these materials, aspiring practitioners cannot be adequately prepared to fully develop the academic talents of college athletes.

Indeed, there is a need and a high consumer demand for teaching tools that better prepare practitioners and others who work directly with college athletes. These professionals need core competencies that equip them to use research and theory to inform their decision-making processes, and to find new and imaginative ways to engage and re-engage college athletes. Thus, this edited volume evolved from the need for a range of viewpoints about and models of data-driven practices in support centers, as well as the absence of a prevailing teaching tool to consolidate baseline knowledge on data-driven best practices.

Making the Connection: Data-Informed Practices in Academic Support Centers for College Athletes is practical and ideal for those who seek to use research to inform their individual and organizational practices. This volume is primarily intended for upper-level undergraduate and graduate students, though scholars, researchers, teachers, practitioners, coaches, athletics administrators, and advocates of intercollegiate athletics will also find it useful. It comprises a series of chapters that cover a wide range of evidence-based approaches designed to enhance the practices of those who work closely with college athletes. Given the breadth of the field overall, this single volume is not exhaustive, but the current concerns, challenges, and themes of relevance to higher education researchers, practitioners, and others are well addressed.

The intent of the text is to spark conversation about how college and university constituents can reframe their thinking about the importance of innovative research to careful, informed practice. Likewise, the contributors hope that it will inspire greater awareness and action among practitioners, as well as advance scholarship in the area of athletics. Each chapter includes current research, and in some cases theoretical perspectives, which should assist practitioners as they enhance the well-being of college athletes. Each chapter also offers guided discussion questions that are ideal as the basis of further classroom conversations.

In Chapter 1, Eddie Comeaux applies organizational learning theory to athletic departments in order to make a case for the Career Transition Scorecard, an anti-deficit and data-driven approach designed to improve the well-being of college athletes. The focus of Chapter 2, written by Joy Gaston Gayles, Rebecca E. Crandall, and Mary Howard-Hamilton, is on using data-informed practices to facilitate college athletes' learning and personal development. Joshua C. Watson's discussion on the indivisible self model of wellness in Chapter 3 offers a potential approach to improving the health and functioning of college athletes. In Chapter 4, Joseph N. Cooper describes a series of effective data-driven strategies that facilitate positive developmental outcomes for college athletes at historically Black colleges and universities. And, in Chapter 5, Whitney Griffin brings greater awareness about sports-related concussions, learning disabilities, and attention-deficit/hyperactivity disorders, and how they impact college athletes. The chapter includes research-informed strategies for improving the well-being of athletes with invisible injuries and deficits.

Chapters 6 through 9 describe empirical studies that have examined particular programs relevant to college athletes. First, C. Keith Harrison and Janet Rasmussen describe Scholar Baller, a culturally relevant and evidence-based program for engaging and re-engaging college athletes. Then, using data from a phenomenological study, Kristina M. Navarro discusses how student affairs professionals can more effectively support and prepare college athletes for quality career transitions after sports. Anne Browning describes a research-driven academic skills intervention through a summer bridge program for "special admit" college athletes. And Laura M. Bernhard and Lydia F. Bell use empirical data to discuss how the physical location of athletic facilities and academic support service centers can impact the quality of experience for college athletes. Finally, in Chapter 10, the volume concludes with Elizabeth Broughton's reflections on expectations and predictions about the future of evidence-based strategies in the academic support for athletes.

Adopters of this text will benefit from leading voices in the field who delve into complex issues, shed new light, and present unique opportunities for understanding a diversity of perspectives on evidence-based practices in support centers for athletes. In all, this volume provides a rich portrait of data-driven practices designed to assist practitioners and others who work closely with college athletes, and it lays the groundwork for an ambitious and long overdue agenda to further develop innovative research that informs the practices of athletics' stakeholders and improves the quality of experiences for college athletes.

ACKNOWLEDGMENTS

Many people have contributed to this volume in significant ways. First, I thank the contributing authors for their dedication, creativity, expertise, and thoughtful chapters, thus making this project a reality. I would also like to thank those colleagues whom I asked for advice and who graciously shared their ideas for this project. I am as well indebted to those at Information Age Publishing who supported the writing of this project. I hope that readers of this volume will find it useful in their own practices.

CHAPTER 1

ORGANIZATIONAL LEARNING IN ATHLETIC DEPARTMENTS

Toward an Anti-Deficit and Data-Driven Approach to Academic Support for Division I Athletes

Eddie Comeaux

ABSTRACT

There are increasing concerns about the educational experiences of Division I athletes in big-time college sports. Calls for reform have come from within colleges and universities and beyond. In this chapter, I describe the current state of academic support centers for athletes and discuss the role of individual practitioners in organizational learning. Next, I examine the concept of cognitive frames and explore how practitioners make sense of the athlete experience and subsequent outcomes. I also introduce the career transition scorecard (CTS), an anti-deficit and data-driven approach, designed to improve the strengths and meet the needs of Division I athletes and to shape and advance the future direction of athletic organizations.

Pressures are mounting for athletic departments to improve academic intervention strategies and to address inequalities in educational outcomes for their Division I athletes (Comeaux, 2013; Harper, Williams, & Blackman, 2013; Southall, Eckard, Nagel, & Hale, 2012). With the National Collegiate Athletic Association (NCAA) Division I academic progress rate (APR) initiative, which is designed to raise the level of academic expectations and eligibility standards for students who participate in team sports, athletic stakeholders have been primarily concerned with ways to implement academic game plans for athletes. The development of successful strategies has been and will continue to be largely contingent upon the processes and approaches that practitioners employ. Indeed, the educational decisions and practices of stakeholders in the affairs of athletics—including directors of athletics, head coaches, and practitioners[1]—will inevitably shape the quality of experiences for athletes.

One of the most glaring factors that contributes to ineffective intervention strategies and inequitable outcomes for athletes by race, ethnicity, gender, and sport, is that practitioners in academic support centers rely to a significant degree on anecdotal information rather than empirical data when they make decisions about the academic needs and futures of athletes (Comeaux, 2012). When practitioners are not engaged in the kind of research that influences their practices, they are less likely to be fully aware of the types and magnitude of academic and personal issues that athletes face (Polkinghorne, 2004), and they are less likely to respond to athletes in meaningful and effective ways. Moreover, in the absence of data-driven practices, practitioners generally rely on assumptions and in some cases develop internalized biases about athletes that too often present them through a deficit lens (Benson, 2000; Comeaux, 2007).

I argue in this chapter that the ongoing academic concerns of Division I athletes primarily constitute an organizational learning problem of practitioners as opposed to an individual learning problem of athletes. An athletic department's shared knowledge, norms, assumptions, and histories shape its practices and culture, and may hinder its stakeholders from developing more effective and responsive intervention strategies, and from producing more equal educational outcomes for Division I athletes by race, ethnicity, gender, and sport. Academic intervention strategies have had limited success because of practitioners' own general understandings of and underlying beliefs about athletes, and their inability to alter their preferred understandings so as to meaningful engage and understand their athletes.

Organizational learning theory can help us to develop a deeper understanding of athletic departments and how they may perpetuate undesirable experiences and outcomes for college athletes. The decisions and practices of these departments reflect common understandings of practitioners and other prominent stakeholders in athletics. These shared "cognitive frames," also known as "frames of reference," "schemata," "orientations," and "mental models," are internal images of external reality that shape individual and collective perspectives and drive action, including how information is gathered and interpreted, how professional judgments are made, and how behavior is understood and explained (Bartunek, 1984; Bolman & Deal, 1991; Gentner & Stevens, 1983). They can provide insight into the resolution of some of the organizational learning problems associated with college athletes, including an over reliance on anecdotal information at the expense of empirical data to inform academic intervention strategies. To reframe practitioners' cognitive processes requires an approach to addressing the strengths and needs of athletes that is both anti-deficit[2] and data-driven (e.g., a focus on gathering and analyzing data in order to make informed decisions).

In the sections that follow, I first describe the current state of academic support centers for athletes and discuss the role of individuals in organizational learning. To date, there is little attention toward understanding how the assumptions, attitudes, and beliefs of practitioners shape their practices and ultimately impact the athlete experience. With that in mind, I examine the concept of cognitive frames and explore how practitioners make sense of the athlete experience and subsequent outcomes. Finally, I introduce the career transition scorecard (CTS), an anti-deficit and data-driven approach designed to improve the strengths and meet the needs of Division I athletes and to shape and advance the future direction of athletic organizations.

ACADEMIC SUPPORT CENTERS FOR ATHLETES

Institutions to some degree realize the incredible demands, expectations, challenges, and stresses that athletes face outside of the classroom as the result of their sports participation. This balancing act requires support for both the personal and academic needs of college athletes. The National Association of Academic Advisors for Athletics (N4A) has served as a liaison between academic and athletic communities at colleges and universities since 1975. With members consisting of academic support and student services personnel, their stated purpose is, "to assist the student athletes in *maintaining their eligibility* [emphasis added] and achieving a viable education leading to graduation" (N4A, 2010). In addition to addressing the academic and counseling needs of college athletes, N4A's efforts have led to the development of other specializations such as sport psychology with a concentration on performance enhancement, and mental health counseling for athletes (Chartrand & Lent, 1987; Miller & Wooten, 1985; Petipas, Buntrock, Van Raalte, & Brewer, 1995).

In 1991, the NCAA implemented bylaw 16.3.1.1, which mandated that member colleges and universities provide general academic counseling and tutoring services to all Division I athletes. As a result, a number of academic advisers, learning specialists, and tutors have been employed in an attempt to develop the skills that athletes need in order to achieve academic, athletic, and personal success. The importance placed on support programs for athletes continues to grow, and athletic departments have more than doubled their spending in academic support over the past decade (Wolverton, 2008).

Despite the stated goals of N4A and the development and expansion of academic support services for athletes over the years, the reality is that these efforts largely consist of new rhetoric and language while they produce the same undesirable results for athletes. As it stands, college athletes, particularly in the revenue-generating sports of football and men's basketball, continue to show lesser forms of academic success than their non-athlete counterparts (Harper et al., 2013; NCAA, 2009; Southall et al., 2012), and female athletes exhibit academic performance considerably better than that of their male counterparts (Simons, Van Rheenen, & Covington, 1999). Blame is placed in part on the lack of effective intervention strategies among practitioners that maximize how students successfully participate in the athletic, social, and academic systems of college (Comeaux & Harrison, 2011).

Above all, new ways of thinking about both the academic conditions of athletes and the organizational problems of athletic departments are rarely discussed and certainly deserve greater attention. The stubbornly persistent problems in athletic departments, particularly the ineffective intervention strategies and inequalities in educational outcomes for athletes by race, ethnicity, gender, and sport can be better understood through the perspective of organizational learning theory.

ORGANIZATIONAL LEARNING THEORY

Over several decades, organizational theory has evolved as an analytical lens for examining the behaviors and interrelationships of members of a given organization. Numerous studies, beginning as early as the 1930s with the work of Chester Barnard (1938, 1968), have offered analysis and insight into organizations and organizing processes, including work on organizational leadership (Pfeffer & Salancik, 1978; Schein, 1992; Selznick, 1957), time motion (Taylor, 1911, 2010), bureaucracy and politics (Aldrich, 1979; Mayes & Allen, 1977; Weber, 1947), as well as structure and power influences in organizations (French & Raven, 1959; Pfeffer, 1981; Mintzberg, 1979). In addition, others have focused on the learning processes within organizations, and specifically the processes through which individual learning directly or indirectly influences organizational learning (Argyris, 1993; Argyris & Schön, 1978; Schein, 1992). Several theoretical models of organizational learning have been developed and debated to understand the link between individual and organizational learning.

Leading organizational theorists Argyris and Schön (1978) assert that organizational learning occurs through individual members of the organization. As new members enter a given organization, they can shape organizational frames (to some degree) by negotiating new norms, values, and behaviors. This theory does not suggest that organizational learning comprises the aggregate of learning acquired by each of its members. Rather, it is a much more complex and dynamic process in that, "organizations, unlike individuals, develop and maintain learning systems that not only influence their immediate members, but are then transmitted to others by way of organization histories and norms" (Fiol & Lyles, 1985, p. 804; see also Argyris & Schön, 1996). To further describe this distinction between individual and organization learning, Hedberg (1981, as cited in Fiol & Lyle, 1985) stated:

> Although organizational learning occurs through individuals, it would be a mistake to conclude that organizational learning is nothing but the cumulative result of their members learning. Members come and go, and leadership changes, but organizations' memories preserve certain behaviors, mental maps, norms, and values over time. (p. 804)

Thus, it is clear that learning begins with the members of an organization, but organizational norms, culture, and histories can shape the learning of individual members. Likewise, learning can occur through the exchange of individual and shared cognitive frames.

With this in mind, the importance of understanding the cognitive processes of practitioners and how they make sense of the athlete experience and subsequent outcomes by race, ethnicity, gender, and sport becomes clear. Likewise, we must view these processes in the context of the broader organization. In athletic departments and, more specifically, academic support centers, organizational learning takes place through individual members and shared organizational practices, norms, and histories. The practices and assumptions of practitioners, as influenced by the organizational culture, can impede or facilitate the learning and personal development of athletes. The next section expands on the notion of cognitive frames to describe the practices and assumptions of practitioners in academic support centers.

SHARED COGNITIVE FRAMES
IN ACADEMIC SUPPORT CENTERS FOR ATHLETES

Cognitive frames or mental models represent the various lenses through which individuals make sense of the world around them. Cognitive frames include knowledge, assumptions, expectations, values, and norms that guide behavior and shape decisions. Kim (1993) asserted, "Mental models not only help us make sense of the world we see, they can also restrict our understanding to that which makes sense within the mental model" (p. 5). Therefore, it is conceivable that assumptions within an individual's cognitive frame could result in supportive or negative judgments and actions in a given situation.

Bensimon (2005) described three types of cognitive frames that institutional actors may use to understand inequalities in educational outcomes for underserved groups: deficit, diversity, and equity. In this section, I focus on the first of these—deficit thinking—to highlight how such a cognitive frame may guide the practices of practitioners in athletic departments, particularly as they relate to standardized measures of athletes' academic progress. I also introduce an anti-deficit and data-driven cognitive frame, which is quite similar to an equity-minded frame, and describe how it can govern the ways in which individuals perceive and interpret the athlete experience.

Because of stringent NCAA rules related to the academic progress rate (APR) initiative, practitioners in academic support centers have increasingly had to understand and explain the extent to which contextual factors (such as course offerings and campus involvement patterns) influence athlete learning and personal development by race, ethnicity, gender, and sport.[3] They are now compelled to provide more supportive environments and responsive intervention strategies for athletes and to monitor their academic production and progress towards their intended degrees. The assumptions and practices of individual practitioners related to these and other efforts are primarily linked to shared cognitive frames formed through socialization with other athletic stakeholders and the organization itself. Their cognitive frames may reflect particular beliefs and assumptions about: (a) how the problems of athletes are defined and solved; (b) how athletes are perceived intellectually by race, ethnicity, gender, and sport; and (c) what approaches should be employed to engage or re-engage athletes academically.

Practitioners who are guided by a deficit cognitive frame may care deeply about the academic well-being of their athletes, but they are likely to ascribe differences in team APR scores and overall academic performance of athletes by race, ethnicity, gender, and sport to cultural stereotypes or alleged internal deficiencies linked to the athletes themselves (e.g., low cognitive ability or a lack of motivation). In other words, academic failure or underperformance is perceived as a problem with the athlete rather than a problem with the college or university system. Practitioners with a deficit-thinking orientation likewise tend to cast the academic underperformance of athletes as generally inevitable, and essentially something beyond their ability to resolve. Lastly, deficit-minded practitioners are more prone to rely on assumptions and anecdotal information to make decisions about the academic strengths and needs of athletes than they are to rely on data (Comeaux, 2013).

In contrast, practitioners who are guided by an anti-deficit and data-driven cognitive frame tend to believe all college athletes are capable of learning. Thus, they deliberately focus on processes and data-driven approaches for enhancing athletes' strengths as well as improving team APR scores and the overall academic success of athletes within all racial and ethnic groups, in both genders, and across all sports. They draw on empirical research findings to identify structural inequalities and institutional policies and practices that affect athletes' academic performance, rather than placing blame on the athletes themselves. They are more inclined to work closely with athletes to understand their backgrounds in order to respond meaningfully to them. Anti-deficit and data-driven practitioners use research to inform decision making and to ask compelling questions. For example, they may seek to understand how individuals from specific racial or ethnic backgrounds, of different genders, or who play different types of sports manage to overcome obstacles or how they engage in meaningful campus relationships, enhance the quality of their experiences, and successfully achieve their desired educational outcomes.

Practitioners in academic support centers are more apt to develop deficit-oriented views than anti-deficit and data-driven cognitive frames of athletes for at least two reasons. First, practitioners primarily focus on merely keeping athletes academically eligible (Knight Commission on Intercollegiate Athletics, 2001), which clearly reinforces the status quo and creates an athletic subculture of low academic expectations. Second, the individual and collective learning in athletic departments are rarely tested or challenged through empirical research. In a survey of advisors and counselors in academic support centers for athletes at Division I colleges and universities, less than 3% of participants reported their programs and services included assessment plans to measure their impact on learning outcomes for athletes (Comeaux, 2012). Data-driven practices coupled with assessment tools to understand how and if program outcomes are being achieved are imperative. Without these components it becomes almost impossible to offer feedback or to identify strengths and performance gaps of athletes, and likewise practitioners are more prone to develop biased, deficit-minded views of athletes (Comeaux, 2007). Toward this end, Bolman and Deal (1997) asserted:

Instructional leaders with narrow, simple, or simple-minded perspectives cannot hope to be consistently successful over the long term. If these perspectives are employed in isolation, it is likely that only on the rare occasion when a situation fits the perspective can true resolution result. In the other cases, misunderstanding, miscommunication and failure are the more likely result. Through reflective analysis of each situation, including the people involved, type of problem, etc., the instructional leader can find clarity and meaning amid the confusion of organizational life. (p. 347)

There is certainly a need for changes in the fundamental ways in which practitioners and other athletic stakeholders learn to think about athletes and differences in their academic outcomes by race, ethnicity, gender, and sport. But the questions remain: How can practitioners in academic support centers reframe their preferred and shared understandings to an anti-deficit and data-driven cognitive frame? How can they view students in new and different ways? How can they begin to understand what processes and approaches will lead to more effective intervention strategies and equitable educational outcomes for athletes of all races, ethnicities, genders, and sport? The next section begins to answer these questions.

FRAMEWORK FOR THE
CAREER TRANSITION SCORECARD (CTS) FOR ATHLETES

Change requires attention to both the individual and the organizational levels, and Argyris and Schön's (1996) single-loop and double-loop learning concepts are especially helpful for shedding light on the relationship between the two. Single-loop learning focuses generally on solving problems, as support centers for athletes have historically done, but fails to address the various factors, including the underlying norms, assumptions, beliefs, and values of the organization, that caused the problems in the first place. By contrast, double-loop learning involves questioning the problems of learning systems, or challenging objectives, assumptions, practices, policies, and norms of a given organization. In double-loop learning, data are used to increase awareness of existing problems, recognize inequalities, promote critical thinking, and challenge underlying cognitive frames. Bensimon (2005) concluded that, "The difference between single-loop and double-loop learning is that in the former, change is at a surface level, whereas in the latter, the change is in underlying norms, beliefs, and principles" (p. 104).

Today's academic support centers will have to forge a more authentically responsive approach to address the needs of intercollegiate athletes in American higher education. This approach must include new and different ways of thinking about all athletes and their academic conditions.

Practitioners and stakeholders alike will need to engage in double-loop learning to address the surface issues and the root causes of inequitable outcomes for athletes. Cognitive processes must shift from a deficit to an anti-deficit and data-driven frame, and organizational problems will need to be understood in sometimes radically different ways. Moreover, evidence-based work must be viewed as a tool for social justice. Only then can the preferred and shared cognitive frame of practitioners in academic support centers for athletes accurately reflect and effectively achieve the desired academic goals and vision of the given athletic department.

One possible approach to shifting cognitive frames among practitioners in academic support centers for athletes, is the career transition score-card (CTS). The CTS and its methodological approach evolved from the diversity scorecard (Bensimon, Polkinghorne, Bauman, & Vallejo, 2004), which has been used to address the opportunity gap for historically under-represented students. The diversity scorecard is based on the assumption that shedding light on the racial patterns in educational outcomes through relevant data can motivate individuals and organizations to seek improvement and change. More precisely, it is premised on the understanding that awareness of inequities leads to informed interpretations of the given situation, which can then lead to action.

Drawing from this general framework, the CTS is designed to help bridge the gap between research and practice in academic support centers for Division I athletes, and to address the lack of explicit and positive learning environments designed to influence desirable educational outcomes of athletes across race, ethnicity, gender, and sport. The CTS is intended not only to shed light on the educational patterns of athletes and to foster evidence-based practices among higher education practitioners, but also to enhance the quality of athletes' school-to-career transitions. Thus, like the diversity scorecard project upon which it is based, the CTS is designed generally to improve educational outcomes for certain student groups and to bring about change at the individual and organizational levels. In Argyris and Schön's (1996) terminology, the CTS operationalizes double-loop learning in the athletic department.

The CTS employs the practitioner-as-researcher model developed by Bensimon and colleagues (2004) as an alternative methodology of knowledge production. "Individuals conduct research about their own institutions, and by doing so they acquire knowledge that they can use to bring about change in these institutions" (p. 108). That is, practitioners within an academic support center for athletes become researchers, and an outside professional researcher takes on the role of facilitator. The facilitator determines the conceptual framework and research agenda, but the practitioner researchers conduct the actual research and assume responsibility for working closely with the facilitator to compile, analyze, and interpret existing data on the athlete campus experience and to develop and implement intervention strategies (i.e., action plans). It is also the responsibility of the practitioner researchers to maintain existing data on the college athlete experience. Unlike in a traditional approach, the CTS methodology provides opportunities for practitioners to construct their own knowledge within their own context, examine their own assumptions about students, and provide new awareness of issues affecting students (Bensimon et al., 2004).

Both the diversity scorecard and the CTS consist of desirable outcomes in the following general areas: access, retention, institutional receptivity, and excellence or high achievement. The CTS also adds an engagement domain (see Figure 1.1). Under the *access* domain, participating athletic departments might begin with existing data that answers thoughtful questions about athletes' access (or lack thereof) to internship opportunities and certain majors, which can influence both their learning and desirable outcomes (Kuh, 2008). The *retention* perspective might focus on the completion rates and levels of success in basic skills courses among athletes. Under the *institutional receptivity* domain, athletic departments might use existing data to answer questions about the extent to which coaches, staff, and administrators reflect the diversity of the athletes they recruit (Comeaux & Fuentes, 2015; Lapchick, Agusta, Kinkopf, & McPhee, 2013). The *excellence or high achievement* perspective on college athletes might begin with existing data that provide answers to questions about participation in high demand programs of study, career placement post graduation, and the types and magnitude of academic honor and awards received. Lastly, the *engagement* domain can bring attention to the interaction patterns of athletes in campus learning environments (Comeaux & Harrison, 2011). Engagement activities can include, but are not limited to, preparing for class, reading and writing, meaningful interactions with faculty, and collaboration with peers on problem solving tasks (Kuh, 2001). With a better understanding of the frequency and quality of athletes' interactions with faculty, for example, practitioners would be more likely and better able to take actions (e.g., establish a faculty-student mentor program) that could lead to positive gains in learning (Comeaux, 2010; Gaston-Gayles & Hu, 2009). In all of this inquiry, it would be particularly prudent for the team of practitioner researchers to explore how all of these aspects of the performance of athletes vary by subgroups (i.e., race, ethnicity, gender, and sport).

Each participating athletic department might have different circumstances, needs, and interests within the CTS framework, and might select specific domains on which to focus. Thus, the professional facilitator works closely with the team of practitioners in the participating athletic departments to build a professional learning community and to help create a version of the CTS that is specific to the institution. After deliberate selection of performance perspectives, the professional facilitator and practitioner

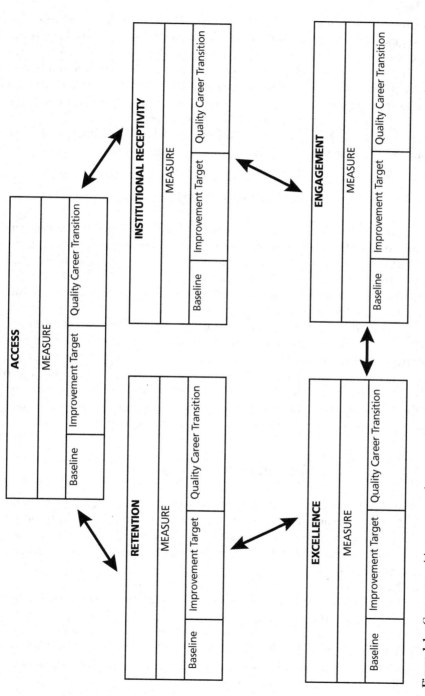

Figure 1.1 Career transition scorecord.

researchers can identify strengths and problem areas and construct tailored goals and measures as well as baselines and improvement targets under each selected domain. This approach will allow the team to assess and evaluate the patterns and conditions of athletes linked to desired outcomes. Through the ongoing process of creating the career transition scorecard and examining the data disaggregated by subgroups, practitioners essentially become knowledge *makers* rather than merely knowledge *users*. In so doing, they have the opportunity to shift their cognitive frames, and think from an anti-deficit and data-driven standpoint.

CONCLUSION

It is clear that understanding the shared cognitive processes of practitioners in support centers is an important first step toward organizational learning, but not sufficient for advancing and achieving organizational learning that is consistent with an athletic organization's desired goals and vision. As such, there is a need to engage in double-loop learning techniques, including using anti-deficit and data driven approaches such as the career transition scorecard to increase awareness of existing problems that challenge underlying cognitive frames of practitioners, and to recognize inequalities among athletes across race, ethnicity, gender, and sport. When understood through a lens that highlights the centrality of organizational learning to positive athlete outcomes, it is evident that practitioners' understandings of the academic conditions of athletes inevitably shape the quality of their campus experiences and subsequent educational outcomes.

QUESTIONS FOR DISCUSSION

1. In what ways can we promote organizational learning among practitioners in academic support centers? How can this learning improve academic intervention strategies and identify and address inequalities in educational outcomes for Division I athletes by race, ethnicity, gender, and sport?
2. In what ways can anti-deficit and data-driven cognitive frames be encouraged among practitioners in academic support centers? What processes and actions might lead practitioners to shift their shared cognitive frame from deficit to anti-deficit and data-driven?
3. What role can faculty and other stakeholders in the affairs of intercollegiate athletics play in the improvement of data-driven practices in academic support centers for athletes?

4. What data collection methods currently exist in support centers for athletes? And how do we know that athletes are developing and learning as students?
5. What incentives can be offered to encourage and improve data-driven practices in academic support centers?
6. What areas of academic support for athletes are in most need of further research?

NOTES

1. Practitioner refers to academic advisors, counselors, staff, tutors, and administrators.
2. See Harper (2010) and Padilla, Trevino, Gonzalez & Trevino (1997) for examples of anti-deficit or success models.
3. The NCAA monitors Division I schools through its academic progress rate (APR) measurement tool, which essentially provides a snapshot of an institution's academic culture, particularly the eligibility, retention, and graduation of its athletes in team sports (NCAA, 2011a). Under the APR system, each athlete earns a maximum of two points, one for maintaining academic eligibility and another for staying in school. The team members' scores are tallied and divided by the total number of possible points, and then multiplied by 1,000, yielding a maximum score of 1,000. Teams that fail to achieve an average APR score of 930 over their last two years are subject to sanctions such as loss of scholarships, reduction in practice times, suspension of coaches, and a ban from post-season competition (NCAA, 2011b).

REFERENCES

Aldrich, H. E. (1979). *Organizations and environments*. Englewood Cliffs, NJ: Prentice Hall.

Argyris, C. (1993). *Knowledge for action: A guide to overcoming barriers to organizational change*. San Francisco, CA: Jossey-Bass.

Argyris, C., & Schön, D. A. (1978). *Organizational learning: A theory of action perspective*. Reading, MA: Addison-Wesley.

Argyris, C., & Schön, D. A. (1996). *Organizational learning II: Theory, method, and practice*. Reading, MA: Addison-Wesley.

Barnard, C. I. (1938/1968). *The functions of the executive*. Cambridge, MA: Harvard University Press.

Bartunek, J. (1984). Changing interpretive schemes and organizational restructuring: The example of a religious order. *Administrative Science Quarterly, 27*, 355–372.

Bensimon, E. M. (2005). Closing the achievement gap in higher education: An organizational learning perspective. In A. J. Kezar (Ed.), *Organizational learning in higher education* (New Directions for Higher Education, No. 131, pp. 99–111). San Francisco, CA: Jossey-Bass.

Bensimon, E. M., Polkinghorne, D. E., Bauman, G., & Vallejo, E. (2004). Doing research that makes a difference. *The Journal of Higher Education, 75*(1), 104–126.

Benson, K. F. (2000). Constructing academic inadequacy: African American athlete's stories of schooling. *Journal of Higher Education, 71,* 223–246.

Bolman, L. G., & Deal, T. E. (1991). *Modern approaches to understanding and managing organizations.* San Francisco, CA: Jossey-Bass.

Bolman, L. G., & Deal, T. E., (1997). Reframing organizations: Artistry, choice, and leadership (2nd ed.). San Francisco, CA: Jossey-Bass.

Chartrand, J. M., & Lent, R. W. (1987). Sports counseling: Enhancing the development of the student athlete. *Journal of Counseling & Development, 66,* 164–167.

Comeaux, E. (2007). Student(less) athlete: Identifying the unidentified college student. *Journal for the Study of Sports and Athletes in Education, 1*(1), 37–43.

Comeaux, E. (2010). Mentoring as an intervention strategy: Toward a (re)negotiation of first year student-athlete role identities. *Journal for the Study of Sports and Athletes in Education, 4*(3), 257–275.

Comeaux, E. (2012). *The role and influence of support service practitioners and big-time college head coaches: An academic-athletic priority collision.* Paper presented at the annual meeting of the American Educational Research Association, Vancouver, Canada.

Comeaux, E. (2013). Rethinking academic reform and encouraging organizational innovation: Implications for stakeholder management in college sports. *Innovative Higher Education, 38,* 281–293.

Comeaux, E., & Fuentes, M. V. (2015). Cross-racial interaction of Division I athletes: An examination of the campus climate for diversity. In E. Comeaux (Ed.), *Introduction to Intercollegiate Athletics* (pp. 179–192). Baltimore, MD: Johns Hopkins University Press.

Comeaux, E., & Harrison, C. K. (2011). A conceptual model of academic success for student athletes. *Educational Researcher, 40,* 235–245.

Fiol, M. C., & Lyles, M. A. (1985). Organizational learning. *Academy of Management Review, 10,* 803–813.

French, J. R. P., Jr., & Raven, B. (1959). The bases of social power. In D. Cartwright (Ed.), *Studies in social power* (pp. 156–165). Ann Arbor, MI: University of Michigan.

Gaston-Gayles, J. L., & Hu, S. (2009). The influence of student engagement and sport participation on college outcomes among Division I student athletes. *Journal of Higher Education, 80,* 315–333.

Gentner, D., & Stevens, A. L. (Eds.). (1983). *Mental models.* Hillsdale, NJ: Erlbaum.

Harper, S. R. (2010). An anti-deficit achievement framework for research on students of color in STEM. In S. R. Harper & C. B. Newman (Eds.), *Students of color in STEM: Engineering a new research agenda* (New Directions for Institutional Research, No. 148, pp. 63–74). San Francisco, CA: Jossey-Bass.

Harper, S. R., Williams, C. D., & Blackman, H. W. (2013). *Black male student-athletes and racial inequities in NCAA Division I college sports.* Philadelphia, PA: University of Pennsylvania, Center for the Study of Race and Equity in Education.

Hedberg, B. (1981). How organizations learn and unlearn. In P. C. Nystrom & W. H. Starbuck (Eds.), *Handbook of organizational design* (pp. 3–27). New York, NY: Oxford University Press.

Kim, D. H. (1993). The link between individual and organizational learning. *Sloan Management Review, 34*(1), 37–50.

Knight Commission on Intercollegiate Athletics (2001). *A call to action: Reconnecting college sport and higher education.* Miami, FL: Author.

Kuh, G. D. (2001). Assessing what really matters to student learning: Inside the national survey of student engagement. *Change, 33*(3), 10–17.

Kuh, G. D. (2008). *High-impact practices: What they are, who has access to them, and why they matter.* Washington, DC: Association of American Colleges and Universities.

Lapchick, R., Agusta, R., Kinkopf, N., & McPhee, F. (2013). *The 2012 racial and gender report card: College sport.* Orlando, FL: University of Central Florida, The Institute for Diversity and Ethics in Sport.

Mayes, B. T., & Allen, R. W. (1977). Toward a definition of organizational politics. *Academy of Management Review, 2,* 672–678.

Miller, C. M., & Wooten, H. R. (1995). Sports counseling: A new counseling specialty area. *Journal of Counseling & Development, 74,* 172–173.

Mintzberg, H. (1979). *The structuring of organizations.* Englewood Cliffs, NJ: Prentice Hall.

National Association of Academic Advisors for Athletics. (2010). Retrieved January 21, 2010, from http://nfoura.org/about/history.php

National Collegiate Athletic Association. (2009). *NCAA Division I graduation success rate (GSR) data.* Retrieved from http://fs.ncaa.org/Docs/newmedia/public/rates/index.html

National Collegiate Athletic Association. (2011a). *NCAA academic reform.* Retrieved from http://www.ncaa.org

National Collegiate Athletic Association. (2011b). *National and sport-group APR averages, trends and penalties.* Retrieved from http://www.ncaa.org

Padilla, R. V., Trevino, J., Gonzalez, K., & Trevino, J. (1997). Developing local models of minority student success in college. *Journal of College Student Development, 38*(2), 125–135.

Petitpas, D. R., Buntrock, C. L., Van Raalte, J. L., & Brewer, B. W. (1995). Counseling athletes: A new specialty in counselor education. *Counselor Education & Supervision, 34,* 214–219.

Pfeffer, J. (1981). *Power in organizations.* Marshfield, MA: Pitman.

Pfeffer J., & Salancik, G. R. (1978). *The external control of organizations: A resource dependence perspective.* New York, NY: Harper & Row.

Polkinghorne, D. E. (2004). *Practice and the human sciences: The case for a judgment based practice of care.* Albany, NY: State University of New York Press.

Schein, E. H. (1992). *Organizational culture and leadership* (2nd ed). San Francisco, CA: Jossey-Bass.

Selznick P. (1957). *Leadership in administration.* New York, NY: Harper & Row.

Simons, H. ,Van Rheenen, D., & Covington, M.V. (1999). Academic motivation and the student athlete. *Journal of College Student Development, 40,* 151–161.

Southall, R. M., Eckard, E. W., Nagel, M. S., & Hale, J. M. (2012). *Adjusted graduation gap report: NCAA Division-I football.* Chapel Hill, NC: College Sport Research Institute.

Taylor, F. W. (1911). *The principles of scientific management.* New York, NY: Harper & Brothers.

Taylor, F. W (2010). *The principles of scientific management.* New York, NY: Cosimo Classics.

Weber, M. (1947). *The theory of social and economic organization* (T. Parsons, Trans.). New York, NY: Free Press.

Wolverton, B. (2008). Rise in fancy academic centers for athletes raises questions of fairness. *The Chronicle of Higher Education.* Retrieved from http://chronicle.com

CHAPTER 2

DATA-DRIVEN PRACTICES FOR IMPROVING LEARNING AND PERSONAL DEVELOPMENT FOR COLLEGE ATHLETES

**Joy Gaston Gayles, Rebecca E. Crandall,
and Mary Howard-Hamilton**

ABSTRACT

There is public concern about the extent to which student athletes experience gains in student learning and personal development in ways similar to their non-athlete peers. This is an issue of national importance as critics continue to question the appropriate role of intercollegiate athletics in higher education. This chapter focuses on using data-informed practices to facilitate student learning and personal development for student athletes. First we discuss what student learning and personal development means, followed by a brief discussion of relevant student-development theories. In addition we discuss college-athlete experiences and academic support programs designed to enhance learning and development, and monitor student athletes' eligibility requirements. We conclude with a brief overview of the literature on gains in

Making the Connection, pages 17–32

learning and personal development for athletes, followed by recommendations for using what we know and understand about this population to inform good practice in advising and counseling this special population of college students.

INTRODUCTION

Are student athletes benefitting from the college experience in ways similar to their non-athlete peers? This question represents an issue of critical importance to public and key constituents of the higher-education community. Some of the harshest critics suggest that student athletes do not benefit from the college experience to the same extent as their peers, and that the goals and values of athletics do not align with the goals and values of higher education (Bowen & Levin, 2003; Shulman & Bowen, 2001). Other research reports that student athletes have made gains in educational outcomes, and that in some instances they have experienced greater gains compared to their non-athlete peers (Gayles & Hu, 2009; Umbach, Palmer, Kuh, & Hannah, 2006). This dilemma speaks to the importance of using the best data available to inform practice and make decisions that maximize student learning and personal development for student athletes.

The purpose of this chapter is to discuss the extant literature on student learning and personal development, with particular focus on using this information to better serve student athletes on college campuses. We begin with a discussion of the importance of student learning and personal development, followed by a review of the empirical literature on college athlete gains in learning and personal development. The chapter concludes with recommendations from the empirical literature for improving the athlete experience in ways that maximize gains in student learning and personal development.

IMPORTANCE OF STUDENT LEARNING AND PERSONAL DEVELOPMENT

Student development and learning are terms widely used in higher education and student affairs. Therefore, it is important to be clear on what these terms mean and how they are connected to the undergraduate college student's experience. In recent years, there has been growing concern about the value of higher education (Pallas, 2011). As tuition increases, the public wants to know what students are learning as a result of attending college and whether it is worth the cost. Important learning outcomes range from critical thinking to problem solving to active and collaborative knowledge acquisition (Astin, 1993; Rhodes & Finley, 2013). A recent report from Hart Research Associates that surveyed over 400 members of the American Association of Colleges & Universities (AAC&U) about learning outcomes in higher education, identified a common set of learning outcomes that include a variety of skills: writing, critical thinking, quantitative reasoning, oral communication, intercultural relations, information literacy, ethical reasoning, civic engagement, application of learning, research skills, and integration of learning (Rhodes & Finley, 2013). Some of the most recent research literature on the experiences of student athletes has focused on examining how student athletes compared to their non-athlete peers relative to these important outcomes of undergraduate education.

In addition to learning, college students are expected to make gains in personal development during the college years. Student development refers to a growth process through which individuals increase their capacity over time to make sense of their experiences in more complex ways (Evans, Forney, Guido, Patton, & Renn, 2010). Along the same lines, Rodgers (1990) defined student development as a way to characterize and describe how students grow, progress, and learn during the college years.

The term student development can be found in the names of administrative positions, campus departments or units, and various programming activities. Thus, student development can take on other meanings in addition to the definitions noted above. First, student development can be interpreted as a philosophy that student-affairs professionals use to guide the practice and the nature of services provided. In addition, student development has a programmatic dynamic, in that it represents what student-affairs professionals do, relative to facilitating positive growth and learning. Third, student development represents an organizational structure for the ways in which we group theory and research on adolescent growth and learning. For example, psychosocial, cognitive structural, moral, and personality, are all developmental domains in which students have the capacity and are expected to grow and learn during the college years. Lastly, student development is practical and provides direction for college administrators in terms of the types of issues and experiences faced by college students. Based on what we know and understand about development during the adolescent years, college administrators can design programs, workshops, services, policies and procedures that create a healthy campus environment for promoting positive growth. Thus, understanding student development theory has important implications for policy and practice. In the next section of this chapter, we will review two of the major families of student development theories: psychosocial and cognitive-structural development.

FAMILIES OF STUDENT DEVELOPMENT THEORIES

As previously mentioned, student-development theories can be broken down and categorized in a myriad of ways. One of the more common approaches is to discuss the theories in terms of families of theories. Families of theories represent a way to group theorists who offer different explanations and interpretations on similar aspects of college student development. For example, psychosocial theories focus on the key developmental tasks that individuals negotiate and grapple with during the college years. Social-identity theories are also under the psychosocial family of theories; however, social-identity theories focus specifically on how individuals from various multicultural backgrounds development a positive sense of self.

Cognitive-structural theories focus on how individuals make meaning of their experiences. Moral development is a subset of cognitive-structural theories that focus specifically on how individuals make meaning concerning moral dilemmas. Finally, typology theories focus on differences in learning styles and personality types. For the purpose of this chapter, we discuss two families of theory: psychosocial and cognitive structural. Many of the most important cognitive and affective outcomes of undergraduate education, particularly for student athletes, are derived from these two families of theories. Further, exhausting the literature on student-development theory is beyond the scope of this chapter.

Psychosocial

Psychosocial theories of development focus primarily on the *what* of student development. These theories highlight various developmental tasks that individuals must resolve around discovering who they are and defining who they want to become. Much of our understanding about adolescent development stems from the work of Erik Erikson (1959), who developed an eight-stage model of lifespan development ranging from birth to death. Erikson's work has served as a foundation for later theories that have focused on development specifically during the adolescent years. Key constructs, such as developmental task and developmental crisis, originate from Erikson's work. According to Erikson, individuals must resolve tasks along a continuum from the very beginning of life until well into the elder years. Further, the epigenetic principle suggests that there is a predetermined unfolding of developmental tasks that individuals negotiate over a lifespan, and how successful individuals are in resolving each task is related to successful resolution of subsequent tasks.

Several theorists have used Erikson's work to focus more specifically on identity development during the adolescent years. The work of scholars such as James Marcia, Ruthellen Josselson, and Arthur Chickering are often cited and used in higher education to better understand the developmental experiences of college students. Marcia's work focused on identity formation during the adolescent years by asking individuals about the extent to which they experienced a development crisis and established commitment along several domains such as religion, occupation, and political affiliation. Based on the findings from his work, Marcia developed a typology that described the identity-formation process based on the extent to which individuals experienced a period of crisis or exploration, and whether or not they made a commitment. Individuals in the achieved status described those who, after having a period of exploration, made a commitment. Foreclosure described those who had made a commitment without having a period of exploration. A common example of foreclosure was when students entered college having committed to a major without exploring the possibility of other majors. Moratorium described those who were actively exploring, but had not yet made a commitment. Finally, diffusion described those who were not actively exploring, and had not made a commitment.

Chickering's seven vectors is a commonly used framework that provides a sense of the developmental tasks that students grapple with during the undergraduate years. These seven vectors represent "major highways" that students travel over the course of their college educational experience (Chickering & Riesser, 1993, p. 35). The term *vector* implies that the seven developmental tasks have magnitude and direction. Developing competence, managing emotions, establishing mature relationships, moving through autonomy toward interdependence, establishing identity, establishing purpose, and developing integrity represent key domains of development. Chickering and Riesser suggested that individuals typically experienced the first four vectors during the early college years and grappled with the later three toward the later years of the college experience. However, there is some evidence to suggest that students experience the later vectors early on in their college experience (Foubert, Nixon, Sisson, & Barnes, 2005).

Cognitive Structural

Cognitive-structural theories focus on *how* individuals make meaning of their experiences and describe how individuals perceive, organize, and evaluate events and experiences that occur in their lives. The early work of Jean Piaget (1950), who studied cognitive development in children, informs the family of cognitive structural theories that focus on how adolescents make meaning of their experiences. Several important constructs that are commonly used to describe how individuals make meaning are derived from Piaget's work. Piaget suggested that individuals made meaning through schemas, which are defined as a set of skills individuals use to explore and make sense of their environment. As individuals develop and mature, the complexity of schemas used to make meaning increased. Increasing the complexity of cognitive schemas occurred through the process of assimilation and accommodation. When individuals encountered new information, they first tried to interpret this new information using their current schema. If it fit, then individuals maintained a sense of equilibrium. However, if the new information did not fit their current way of thinking and processing, a sense of cognitive conflict resulted. Cognitive conflict causes us to question our current way of thinking about why new information does not fit. In order to resolve cognitive conflict, individuals adapted their current schema by developing a more complex way of making meaning: This process was called accommodation. For example, a young child learning about animals might learn to recognize characteristics of their pet dog. When the child sees a cow, he or she might first call it a "dog," because it too has four legs. Conflict for the child comes from the parent telling the child that the animal is a cow and not a dog. In order to resolve this conflict, the child has to increase his or her level of cognitive complexity to be able to distinguish between four-legged animals and understand that all four-legged animals are not dogs.

The process of assimilation and accommodation is an important process that cuts across the most commonly-cited cognitive structural theories. William Perry's scheme of cognitive-structural development during the adolescent years was derived from Piaget's work on cognitive development in children. Perry's scheme consists of nine positions of cognitive development that can be grouped into four broad categories: dualism, multiplicity, relativism, and relativism in commitment. Dualism (positions 1 and 2) describes a dichotomous meaning-making process with all questions having a right or wrong answer. In early dualism, there is no concept of multiple realities: Every question or problem has a right or wrong answer and authorities (e.g., teachers, parents, experts) have the right answers. Multiplicity (positions 3 and 4) is characterized as individuals beginning to have a sense that multiple realities exist in some areas, but the *right answer* exists in most domains and can be found in other domains beside authorities. It is not until the relativism (positions 5 and 6) that individuals become comfortable with the notion that uncertainty exists across many domains and that there is a process for evaluating knowledge claims. Within position 6, individuals begin to learn and use the process of evaluating multiple points of view and make a strong argument for one claim over another that is supported by the evidence to date. Positions 7, 8, and 9 of Perry's scheme deals more with making commitments based on evaluating knowledge, which is more characteristic of psychosocial development as opposed to cognitive-structural development.

COLLEGE-ATHLETE EXPERIENCES
AND ACADEMIC-SUPPORT PROGRAMS

Student athletes represent a special population of college students, particularly at the Division I level. Like all students, student athletes wrestle with cognitive and affective developmental tasks and must adjust to life as a college student. In addition to the challenges and developmental tasks faced by all adolescents, student athletes have an additional set of challenges that are unique to the athlete experience (Jordan & Denson, 1990; Parham, 1993; Watt & Moore, 2001). The demands of participating in college sports are quite strenuous and require a huge investment of a student's time and energy. In fact, balancing academic, athletic, and social demands are areas in which student athletes struggle quite a bit (Adler & Adler, 1991). Further, dealing with issues associated with academic and social isolation, which are derived from long hours of practice and long athletic seasons, are not conducive to learning and personal development (Astin, 1993). There are also emotional consequences that result from participating in college sports, such as maintaining one's physical health, dealing with winning and losing, and managing relationships between coaches, parents, teammates, and the community. Attending practice 20 hr a week, traveling, competing, and dealing with injuries are also issues that student athletes face in addition to attending classes and keeping up with academic requirements. Finally, at some point, student athletes must consider the idea of terminating their athletic career, which can be an emotionally-charged experience, particularly considering the likelihood that sports has been a major aspect of their identity since youth. These additional challenges that student athletes face have been documented over the past three decades, and they can complicate and have serious implications for an athlete's development in cognitive and affective domains if not properly addressed.

The College Athlete Experience

Several scholars have written about student athletes' experiences balancing academic, athletic, and social experiences in college (Adler & Adler, 1991; Gaston-Gayles, 2004; Parham, 1993; Settles, Sellers, & Damas, 2002). Balancing the demands of sports, academic, and social life is probably one of the most stressful experiences student athletes face other than game day and exam day. In fact, balancing these demands is even more stressful for students who enter college academically underprepared, or who are first-generation students unsure about what to expect from the college experience.

In the early 1990s, Adler and Adler (1991) studied the experiences of college basketball players and coined the term *role engulfment* that captures the difficulty student athletes experience trying to balance academic and athletic-related tasks. They found that student athletes in their study became over involved in the athletic domain, which left little to no time to devote to academic and social experiences. In fact, the authors found that student athletes actually entered college with high aspirations for their academic experience in college; however, the demands of playing sports led to role engulfment as early as their first or second semester of college.

Other scholars have written about the role-engulfment phenomenon. Parham (1993) found that student athletes in his study experienced issues of balancing academic and athletic tasks; social isolation from so much athletic success; lack of success maintaining physical health and injuries; relationship demands among competing groups such as parents, coaches and friends; and mental well-being from dealing with the emotional strain from winning and losing.

Academic Support and Advising

Since the early 1980s, the NCAA has enforced several rules and regulations to help ensure the academic success of student athletes. Division I athletic programs are required to provide academic support services for student athletes; athletic academic advisors play an important role in the lives of student athletes. Athletic advisors help student athletes maintain balance between academic and athletic priorities to achieve success both on and off the playing field or court (Thompson & Gilchrist, 2011). Academic advisors for student athletes are responsible for monitoring eligibility and grades, as well as checking class attendance. In addition, advisors assist with planning class schedules, finding tutors, and linking student athletes to other academic support services and referrals (both on and off campus) so as to increase academic success.

One of the challenges faced by academic advisors is motivating student athletes to comply with academic responsibilities, such as meeting with tutors, attending study hall, going to class regularly, and meeting with their advisors. For various reasons (e.g., injured, tired, embarrassed, unmotivated), some student athletes resist adhering to academic obligations. Thompson & Gilchrist (2011) explored compliance-gaining strategies for student athletes and examined effective ways in which academic advisors should communicate with student athletes to increase compliance. The authors found that student athletes were most likely to be persuaded by the majority of compliance-gaining strategies, with the exception of negative compliance-gaining strategies, particularly negative altercasting and negative self-feeling. Further, the authors found that student athletes in the study did not consider the strategies differently across the three situations: seeking a tutor, going to class, and meeting with their advisor. An important finding from this study was that academic advisors should consider the context of the situation when trying to gain compliance from students using negative strategies, and to understand when certain strategies are acceptable and unacceptable. For instance, it was more acceptable for advisors to use negative strategies that attack a student athletes' character for not attending class, but it was unacceptable to use such strategies for not seeking out or attending a meeting with a tutor. In other words, making students "feel bad" about missing class is different from making them "feel bad" about needing and missing an appointment with a tutor. Moreover, the first scenario is more likely to result in them attending class, whereas the later will likely lower their self-confidence and thus lower their academic performance.

STUDENT ATHLETES' LEARNING AND PERSONAL DEVELOPMENT

During the 1980s when rules and regulations were instituted to hold student athletes accountable for their academic performance, scholars began examining how participation in college sports impacted student learning and personal development. In particular, there was great interest in the extent to which athletes benefited in ways similar to their non-athlete peers. In addition, scholars were interested in the role that participation in college sports played in explaining differences in cognitive and affective development outcomes between athletes and non athletes.

Involvement and Engagement

Involvement within the college experience has been linked to key outcomes of undergraduate education, such as greater satisfaction with the college experience and gains in academic success (Astin, 1983). In essence, involvement refers to the amount of psychological and physical energy students invest in the college experience. Examples include investment through participation in student groups and organizations, and interacting with faculty and peers. Given the nature of intercollegiate athletics and the athlete experience, there is concern that student athletes may not experience such interactions due to the amount of time and energy dedicated to participating in their sport. A few recent studies have examined this issue empirically and found that, for the most part, student athletes are just as engaged in the college experience as their non-athlete peers (Gayles & Hu, 2009; Umbach, et al., 2006). Umbach, et al., also found that student athletes were more likely to engage with faculty and participate in collaborative learning activities compared to their non-athlete peers. One shortcoming of this study was the inability to account for the type of sport. Other evidence suggested that experiences may differ by type of sport. For instance, Gayles and Hu (2009) found that interacting with non-athlete peers was the most frequently and influential form of involvement for student athletes. Yet, student athletes in high-profile sports (e.g., men's basketball and football) actually reported lower levels of interaction with their non-athlete peers. More research is needed to better understand the types of college experiences that are the most influential for student athletes in all sports.

Cognitive Outcomes

Clear academic deficiencies appear when comparing student athletes to their non-athlete counterparts, which elicits a great deal of concern about the academic performance of student athletes. Every year, the NCAA posts graduation rates for student athletes, which is an indication of how student athletes are matriculating through college and whether they complete a college degree in a timely fashion. The NCAA began reporting graduation rates in the 1980s as a part of the Student Right-To-Know Act. Since that time, scholars have shown interest in the academic performance of student athletes and in potential explanations for low graduation rates for particular groups of student athletes.

Course grades have been criticized for their *relativistic quality* (Astin & Lising Antonio, 2012, p. 12) and inability to provide an accurate representation of the amount of learning that has taken place in a course (Astin & Lising Antonio, 2012). Yet, grade-point averaging remains the most common measurement of academic achievement (Astin & Lising Antonio, 2012). As such, the existence of academic performance gaps for intercollegiate athletes as measured by grade-point averaging is worth noting.

Academic performance disparities for student athletes have been found on a variety of levels, both individual and institutional. In general, Division I student athletes fall behind their non-athlete counterparts in terms of academic success (Eitzen, 2009; Gaston-Gayles, 2004; Lucas & Lovaglia, 2002; Pascarella, Truckenmiller, Nora, Terenzini, Edison, & Hagedorn, 1999). Race, ethnicity, gender, and sport have also emerged as predictors of success in a number of academic performance studies, providing further insight into the often-nuanced nature of academic success for this student population. Gaps are apparent between White and minority athletes (Comeaux, 2008; Eitzen, 1987; Sellers, 1992; NCAA, 2013), with male Division I athletes on high-profile sports teams appearing to be particularly at risk (Comeaux, 2008; Eitzen, 1987).

Beyond simple measures of academic performance, a few scholars have investigated the effect of college athletics on "objective, standardized tests of critical thinking" (Pascarella & Terenzini, 2005, p. 191). In their study utilizing the New Jersey Test of Reasoning Skills and the California Critical Thinking Dispositions Inventory, McBride and Reed (1998) observed outcomes mirroring the general patterns of GPA data. Student athletes exhibited lower levels of critical-thinking ability and less proclivity to use critical-thinking skills than the general student population (McBride & Reed, 1998; Pascarella & Terenzini, 2005). As was the case with GPA research, male revenue-sport athletes appeared to be the most deficient (McBride & Reed, 1998; Pascarella & Terenzini, 2005).

Designs of later studies (Pascarella, Bohr, Nora, & Terenzini, 1995; Pascarella, Truckenmiller, Nora, Terenzini, Edison, & Hagedorn, 1999) included statistical controls that provided a clearer depiction of athletic participation's impact. In their analysis of cognitive outcomes for the first year of college, Pascarella, Bohr, et al. found no notable differences between the critical thinking of student athletes and non athletes of either gender, regardless of the sport revenue level. A follow-up study, aimed at measuring whether the effects continued past the first year of college, again revealed only statistically non-significant effects of athletic participation on critical thinking measures for female and non-revenue sport male athletes. Noteworthy negative effects of athletic participation were discovered for male football and basketball players, however, with critical thinking declines appearing regardless of individual characteristics, athletic division level, or an institution's academic selectivity (Pascarella, Truckenmiller, et al.).

Affective Outcomes

Framed within the identity-development theories of Erikson (1959) and Marcia (1966), as well as Chickering and Reisser's vectors (1993), many studies point to identity foreclosure as a common occurrence for many college athletes. Taking place when one commits to a role "without engaging in exploratory behavior" (Murphy, Petitpas, & Brewer, 1996, p. 240), identity foreclosure is common for athletes whose weekly schedules often involve spending an average of 40–50 hr a week on their sport (Moreland-Bishop, 2009). The struggle to balance the dual roles of student and athlete appears to be a constant reality for students who participate in intercollegiate athletics (Street, 1999).

The identity foreclosure often experienced by athletes is a distinct trait of their population. When comparing athletes to fine-arts students, a student population also required to balance dual roles, McQuown Linnemeyer and Brown (2010) found higher levels of identity foreclosure in student athletes than either general college students or dual-role fine arts students. Their findings seem to parallel those of earlier researchers who contend that athletic identity foreclosure is, in part, prompted by limitations in *exploratory behavior* (McQuown Linnemeyer & Brown, p. 628) on the part of intercollegiate athletes (Chartrand & Lent, 1987; Miller & Kerr, 2002; Petitpas & Champagne, 1988).

The level to which an athlete ascribes to their athletic identity determines the way in which they set their priorities (Coakley, 2001; Comeaux & Harrison, 2011). Adler and Adler (1987), while studying male athletes on revenue-sport teams, noted the way in which priorities often shifted in a way that hindered academic success. In general, they discovered that athletes, regardless of playing time, identified primarily as an athlete (Adler & Adler). Accordingly, when role conflict arose out of competing time commitments, athletes found resolution only by "realigning, reducing, or in extreme cases, dropping their academic role" (Adler & Adler, p. 451). Only then were the athletes able to cope with all of the competing demands.

Many early studies focused on career maturity for student athletes, trying to tease out differences across athletic status, gender, and race or ethnicity. When compared to the general student body, college athletes had lower levels of career maturity (McQuown Linnemeyer & Brown, 2010). Scholars also note the way in which the extreme focus placed on athletic identity limited student athletes' ability to gain a wide range of career-shaping experiences (Good, Brewer, Van Raalte, & Mahar, 1993; Harris, 1993; McQuown Linnemeyer & Brown, 2010; Murphy, Petitpas, & Brewer, 1996).

Although the affective development of student athletes seems to be stymied in the areas of student identity and career maturity, Wolniak, Pierson, and Pascarella's (2001) study on attitudes related to learning for male intercollegiate athletes revealed interesting trends in the area of self-understanding. Statistical controls were included to allow the researchers to examine the effect of collegiate athletic participation on "the value they attached to learning and academic experiences that increased self-understanding" (Pascarella & Terenzini, 2005). Whereas non-revenue sport athletes did increase somewhat in the level of value that they placed on that type of learning over a 3 year period, the value that revenue-sport athletes placed on self-understanding-producing educational experiences was higher. In this area, male basketball and football players not only surpassed their non-revenue sport peers, but they were comparable to the general student population (Pascarella & Terenzini, 2005; Wolniak, Pierson, & Pascarella, 2001).

RECOMMENDATIONS FOR IMPROVING
THE COLLEGE ATHLETE EXPERIENCE

Today, more so than any other period in the history of higher education in the United States, we know from scores of empirical evidence more about how college impacts students. Pascarella and Terenzini (1991, 2005) have produced two volumes of empirical evidence on how students learn and develop during the college years. From this growing body of literature, we also know more about how participation in intercollegiate athletics influences important outcomes of undergraduate education. As a result, athletic administrators can be more intentional about using theory in practice and using practice to inform theory. When thinking about how to maximize student athletes' learning and personal development, athletic administrators have a wealth of empirical literature to draw upon. For example, administrators who advise and counsel student athletes might consider how student-development theory could help student athletes make gains in personal and cognitive development.

Athletic administrators must also consider what important undergraduate outcomes should be for student athletes, given the academic, athletic, and social demands on their time and energy. As opposed to being driven by eligibility requirements and other mandates, a more integrated and *a priori* approach to advising and counseling that focuses on learning and personal development might work better. The idea here is that by focusing more broadly on student learning and personal development outcomes, student athletes can meet eligibility and also make progress toward their degrees.

Once athletic departments decide on the most important learning and personal development outcomes for student athletes, then consideration should be given to the extent to which current programs and services map onto the learning and personal development outcomes identified. In other words, how do the programs and services facilitate learning and personal development. If the answer to this question is unclear, then perhaps redesigning programs and services with the intent of facilitating personal development and student learning is warranted.

Research supports the idea that students are an important source of learning and development (Astin, 1993; Pascarella & Terenzini, 1991, 2005). In other words, a great deal of learning and development takes place from interacting and engaging with other students. Thus, the importance of engaging with one's peers cannot be emphasized enough. Athletic departments should be intentional about finding ways for student athletes to interact with their non-athlete peers. This is fairly easy to do because many of the services and programs offered for student athletes are also offered for all students. Where appropriate, athletic departments can partner with campus offices to cosponsor a program that will benefit students and student athletes alike. Further, doing so avoids unnecessary duplication of services, facilitates sharing of ideas and information that can be useful for everyone, and gives student athletes the opportunity to interact with their non-athlete peers.

QUESTIONS FOR DISCUSSION

1. Psychosocial development focuses on key developmental tasks that individuals negotiate to discover their identities. In what ways might being a college athlete influence the identity-development process during the adolescent years?
2. Since a great deal of learning and development takes place from interacting and engaging with other students, how might a more balanced approach to college-athlete socialization facilitate the development of student athletes?
3. What do you perceive are some of the biggest challenges in fostering the development of student athletes within your specific campus environment? What are some of the areas in which there is great opportunity?

REFERENCES

Adler, P., & Adler, P. A. (1987). Role conflict and identity salience: College athletics and the academic role. *The Social Science Journal, 24,* 443–455.

Adler, P., & Adler, P. A. (1991). *Backboards & blackboards: College athletics and role engulfment.* New York, NY: Columbia University Press.

Astin, A. W. (1993). *Assessment for excellence.* Phoenix: American Council on Education & The Oryx Press.

Astin, A. W. (1993). *What matters in college? Four critical years revisited.* San Francisco, CA: Jossey-Bass.

Astin, A. W., & Lising Antonio, A. (2012). *Assessment for excellence* (2nd ed.). Lanham, MD: Rowman & Littlefield.

Bowen, W. G., & Levin, S. A. (2011). *Reclaiming the game: College sports and educational values.* Princeton, NJ: Princeton University Press.

Chartrand, J., & Lent, R. (1987). Sports counseling: Enhancing the development of the athlete. *Journal of Counseling and Development, 66,* 164–167.

Chickering, A. W., & Reisser, L. (1993). *Education and identity* (2nd ed.). San Francisco, CA: Jossey-Bass.

Coakley, J. (2001). *Sport in society.* Boston, MA: McGraw-Hill.

Comeaux, E. (2008). Black males in the college classroom: A quantitative analysis of student athlete-faculty interactions. *Challenge, 14*(1), 1–13.

Comeaux, E., & Harrison, C. K. (2011). A conceptual model of academic success for student athletes. *Educational Researcher, 40*(5), 235–245. doi: 10.3102/0013189X11415260

Eitzen, D. (1987). The educational experiences of intercollegiate student athletes. *Journal of Sport and Social Issues, 11*(15), 15–30. doi: 10.1177/019372358701100102

Eitzen, D. (2009). *Fair and foul: Beyond the myths and paradoxes of sport.* New York, NY: Rowman & Littlefield.

Erikson, E. (1959). Identity and the life cycle: Selected papers. *Psychology Issues, 1*(1), 5–165.

Evans, N. J., Forney, D. S., Guido, F. M., Patton, L. D., & Renn, K. A. (2010). *Student development in college: Theory, research, and practice.* San Francisco, CA: Jossey-Bass.

Foubert, J. D., Nixon, M., Sisson, S., & Barners, A. B. (2005). A longitudinal study of Chickering and Reisser's vectors: Exploring gender differences and implications for refining the theory. *Journal of College Student Development, 46,* 461–471.

Gaston-Gayles, J. L. (2004). Examining academic and athletic motivation among student athletes at a Division I university. *Journal of College Student Development, 45*(1), 75–83. doi: 10.1353/csd.2004.0005

Gayles, J. G., & Hu, S. (2009). The influence of student engagement and sport participation on college outcomes among Division I student athletes. *The Journal of Higher Education, 80*(3), 315–333.

Good, A. J., Brewer, B. W., Petitpas, A. J., Van Raalte, J. L., & Mahar, M. T. (1993) Identity foreclosure, athletic identity, and college sport participation. *Academic Athletic Journal, 8,* 1–12.

Harris, M. M. (1993). Developmental benefits of athletics. In W. D. Kirk & S. V. Kirk (Eds.), *Student athletes: Shattering the myths & sharing the realities* (pp. 3–11). Alexandria, VA: American Counseling Association.

Jordan, J. M., & Denson, E. L. (1990). Student services for athletes: A model for enhancing the student-athlete experience. *Journal of Counseling & Development, 69*(1), 95–97.

Lucas, J. W., & Lovaglia, M. J. (2002). Athletes' expectations for success in athletics compared to academic competition. *The Sport Journal, 5*(2). Retrieved from http://www.thesportjournal.org/article/athletes-expectations-success -athletics-compared-academic-competition

Marcia, J. E. (1966). Development and validation of ego-identity status. *Journal of Personality and Social Psychology, 5,* 551–558.

McBride, R., & Reed, J. (1998). Thinking and college athletes: Are they predisposed to critical thinking? *College Student Journal, 32*(3), 443–450.

McQuown Linnemeyer, R., & Brown, C. (2010). Career maturity and foreclosure in student athletes, fine arts students, and general college students. *Journal of Career Development, 37*(3), 616–634. doi: 10.1177/0894845309357049

Miller, P. S., & Kerr, G. (2002). The athletic, academic, and social experiences of intercollegiate student athletes. *Journal of Sport Behavior, 25*(4), 346–368.

Moreland-Bishop, L. (2009). *The impact of transition out of intercollegiate athletics* (Doctoral dissertation). Retrieved from ProQuest Digital Dissertations. (UMI 3369270)

Murphy, G. M., Petitpas, A. J., & Brewer, B. W. (1996). Identity foreclosure, athletic identity, and career maturity in intercollegiate athletics. *The Sport Psychologist,* (10), 239–246.

National Collegiate Athletic Association (2013). *Trends in graduation-success rates and federal graduation rates at NCAA Division I institutions* [PDF document]. Retrieved from http://www.ncaa.org/sites/default/files/ GSR%2Band%2BFed%2BTrends%2B2013_Final_0.pdf

Pallas, A. M. (2011). Assessing the future of higher education. *Society, 48*(3), 213–215.

Parham, W. D. (1993). The intercollegiate athlete: A 1990s profile. *The Counseling Psychologist, 21*(3), 411–429.

Pascarella, E., Bohr, L., Nora, A., & Terenzini, P. (1995). Intercollegiate athletic participation and freshman-year cognitive outcomes. *Journal of Higher Education, 66*(4), 369–387. Retrieved from http://www.jstor.org/stable/2943793

Pascarella, E., & Terenzini, P. (1991). *How college affects students: Findings and insights from twenty years of research.* San Francisco, CA: Jossey-Bass.

Pascarella, E., & Terenzini, P. (2005). *How college affects students (Vol. 2): A third decade of research.* San Francisco, CA: Jossey-Bass.

Pascarella, E. T., Truckenmiller, R., Nora, A., Terenzini, P. T., Edison, M., & Hagedorn, L. S. (1999). Cognitive impacts of intercollegiate athletic participation: Some further evidence. *The Journal of Higher Education, 70*(1), 1–26. Retrieved from http://www.jstor.org/stable/2649116

Petitpas, A. J., & Champaign, D. E. (1988). Developmental programming for intercollegiate athletes. *Journal of College Student Development, 29*(5), 454–460.

Piaget, J. (1950). *The psychology of intelligence.* Orlando, FL: Harcourt Brace Jovanovich.

Rhodes, T., & Finley, A. (2013). *Using the VALUE rubrics for improvement of learning and authentic assessment.* Washington, DC: Association of American Colleges and Universities.

Rodgers, R. F. (1990). Recent theories and research underlying student development. *College Student Development, 49,* 27–79.

Sellers, R. M. (1992). Racial differences in the predictors for academic achievement of student athletes in Division I revenue producing sports. *Sociology of Sport Journal, 9*(1), 48–59.

Settles, I. H., Sellers, R. M., & Damas, A. Jr. (2002). One role or two?: The function of psychological separation in role conflict. *Journal of Applied Psychology, 87*(3), 574.

Shulman, J. L., & Bowen, W. G. (2011). *The game of life: College sports and educational values.* Princeton, NJ: Princeton University Press.

Street, J. M. (1999). Self-efficacy: A tool for providing effective support services for student athletes. In S. Robinson (Ed.), *Gaining the competitive edge: Enriching the collegiate experience of the new student-athlete.* Columbia, NC: National Resource Center for the First Year Experience and Students in Transition, University of South Carolina.

Thompson, J., & Gilchrist, E. (2011). The academic advisor's playbook: Seeking compliance from college student athletes. *NACADA Journal, 31*(1), 29–41.

Umbach, P. D., Palmer, M. M., Kuh, G. D., & Hannah, S. J. (2006). Intercollegiate athletes and effective educational practices: Winning combination or losing effort? *Research in Higher Education, 47,* 709–733.

Watt, S. K., & Moore, J. L. (2001). Who are student athletes? *New Directions for Student Services,* (93), 7–18.

Wolniak, G., Pierson, C., & Pascarella, E. (2001). Effects of intercollegiate athletic participation on male orientations toward learning. *Journal of College Student Development, 42,* 604–624.

CHAPTER 3

A HOLISTIC WELLNESS APPROACH TOWARD COUNSELING COLLEGE ATHLETES

Joshua C. Watson

ABSTRACT

Each year over 400,000 students participate in intercollegiate athletic programs sanctioned by the National Collegiate Athletic Association (NCAA, 2012). For many of these students, their experiences are positive and the memories they take from their time as student athletes last a lifetime. For others, their experience paints a different story. An estimated 10%–15% of college athletes will exhibit signs and symptoms indicative of mental health problems, which rise to the level of warranting help from a professional counselor, as a result of their role as an athlete (Hinkle, 1994; Murray, 1997; Parham, 1993). In these cases, the challenges of balancing the demands associated with being a student and an athlete, as well as the normal developmental issues associated with young adulthood, can have a deleterious effect on a student's physical and mental health. In this chapter the Indivisible Self Model of Wellness (IS-WEL) is introduced as a potential treatment approach to use when working with athletes. Consistent with many student development models, the IS-WEL can be useful in helping athletes address the many chal-

Making the Connection, pages 33–46
Copyright © 2015 by Information Age Publishing

lenges in their lives and enhance their overall collegiate athletic experience. Conceptually, the IS-WEL is a strength-based, choice-oriented, multidimensional approach that emphasizes the interconnectedness of various dimensions of an individual's life (Myers & Sweeney, 2004). Counselors who apply this model are able to identify individuals' strengths in particular dimensions and use these strengths to improve functioning and overcome deficiencies in other dimensions; this allows them to help their athletes and clients create positive change in their lives.

A HOLISTIC WELLNESS APPROACH
TOWARD COUNSELING COLLEGE ATHLETES

Each year the number of students participating in intercollegiate athletic programs increases. According to the most recent statistics released by the National Collegiate Athletic Association (NCAA; 2012), a total of 430,301 athletes competed in intercollegiate athletic programs on the campuses of the NCAA's 1,066 member institutions during 2009–2010. For the vast majority of these athletes, their participation in intercollegiate athletics is the fulfillment of a childhood dream. The experience is one that will create for them many fond memories and forge friendships that will last a lifetime. However, despite the many positive aspects associated with athletic participation, the athlete experience is not devoid of its challenges and struggles. For some athletes, the task of balancing the multiple demands of being both a student and an athlete may have deleterious effects on both their physical and mental health. As a result, a focus for those support staff personnel working with athletes should be to adopt a holistic perspective to the services they provide. In this chapter you will learn how programs and interventions designed to foster well-being and develop the whole person will help athletes successfully manage the myriad of challenges they will face as they matriculate through college and beyond.

Stress and the Collegiate Experience

According to recent research, a growing number of students perceive their college years to be a stressful experience. In 2012, the American College Health Association (ACHA) conducted a study in which they surveyed over 90,000 college students nationwide regarding their habits, behaviors, and perceptions about the most prevalent health issues on college campuses at that time. The results of their study indicated that the college experience was a challenging and stressful time for a great number of students from all demographic backgrounds. A review of the executive summary released showed that 42.9% of the college students surveyed reported feeling more than an average amount of stress within the previous 12 months. In addition, 86.1% reported feeling overwhelmed by all they had to do and 45.3% felt things were hopeless during the previous 12 months. Consequently, more than 25% of the students surveyed reported being diagnosed or treated by a mental health professional within the previous year. While these numbers provide a snapshot view of what is occurring on college campuses, they reflect a growing trend. In the 2010 national survey of counseling center directors, respondents reported that 44% of the students they saw were seeking treatment for psychological problems that would be categorized as severe. By contrast, respondents in the same survey administered in 2000 reported that only 16% of their clients sought treatment for severe psychological problems (APA, 2013).

Among athletes, these numbers would be expected to be greater. In addition to the myriad of challenges their peers face, athletes must also manage the additional stress and pressure associated with their participation in athletic programs (Broughton & Neyer, 2001). As a result, athletes often are perceived to be a special at-risk group of students more susceptible to mental distress (Watson, 2005). While empirical data has not formally been collected, previous researchers (Hinkle, 1994; Murray, 1997; Parham, 1993) conservatively have estimated that 10%–15% of athletes will exhibit signs and symptoms indicative of mental health problems that rise to the level of warranting help from a professional counselor as a result of their role as a student athlete. To help ameliorate the negative impact stress has on the lives of athletes, a holistic wellness approach focused on the development of the student athlete as a total person might prove useful to those working in a supportive capacity with this unique population.

COUNSELING FOR WELLNESS

Conceptually, wellness models are a close fit with the college student development models most often employed on today's campuses. Whereas previous wellness models focused primarily on physical health, a new paradigm of wellness emerged during the 1990s "as an alternative to the traditional, illness-based medical model for treatment of mental and physical disorders" (Myers, Sweeney, & Witmer, 2000, p. 251). This holistic model aims to develop the whole person and to enhance the overall college student experience. The term *wellness* is now most frequently associated on college and university campuses with programs designed to increase the health and well-being of the student population (Granello, 1999). In these programs, wellness is best understood as a multidimensional approach in which mind, body, and spirit are integrated in a purposeful manner with a goal of living life more fully (Myers, Sweeney, & Witmer, 2000). In other words, wellness is not defined simply by the absence of disease, but also by the presence of physical, psychological, and spiritual well-being (Myers, 1992; Witmer & Sweeney, 1992). Because counselors who adhere to holistic wellness models are more likely to find themselves well positioned to promote the full functioning of the clients they serve (Carney, 2007) the approach is becoming a popular treatment strategy to employ.

Over the past 25 years there have been several models of holistic wellness developed for use in working with various populations across multiple settings. In each of these models, various components or characteristics of healthy persons that are deemed essential to achieving optimal functioning are presented. Among these various wellness models, the Indivisible Self Model of Wellness (IS-WEL) stands out for its ability to promote improved student health and functioning (Osborn, 2005). At its core, the IS-WEL is a strength-based, choice-oriented, multidimensional approach that emphasizes the interconnectedness of various dimensions of an individual's life. A growing body of literature supporting the efficacy of this model can be found in the professional counseling literature (Myers & Sweeney, 2008). To see how the model may prove useful in working with athletes, let us first examine the structure of the model and how it conceptualizes wellness.

Indivisible Self Model of Wellness (IS-WEL)

The Indivisible Self Model of Wellness (IS-WEL) is an evidence-based, multitiered model of wellness that can be used to assess individual needs, conceptualize issues developmentally, and plan interventions to remediate dysfunction and optimize growth (Myers & Sweeney, 2008). A series of statistical analyses performed by Hattie, Myers, and Sweeney (2004) on the database of wellness information collected by Myers using four early versions of the wellness evaluation of lifestyle (WEL) questionnaire led to the development of the IS-WEL model. The model is comprised of three tiers: a single higher-order wellness factor, 5 second-order wellness factors, and 17 third-order wellness factors (see Figure 3.1). Holistic in nature, the model posits that people are more than the simple sum of their individual parts. In addition, the model promotes the contextual nature of human functioning. As noted by Myers and Sweeney (2005), individuals are both affected by and have an effect on their environment. Because the third-order factors were identified in previous research and are included as the individual components comprising each of the second-order factors defined below, additional information on them is not included in this chapter.

THE INDIVISIBLE SELF:
An Evidence-Based Model of Wellness

CONTEXTS:

Local (safety)
Family
Neighborhood
Community

Institutional (policies & laws)
Education
Religion
Government
Business/industry

Global (world events)
Politics
Culture
Global Events
Environment
Media
Community

Chronometrical (lifespan)
Perpetual
Positive
Purposeful

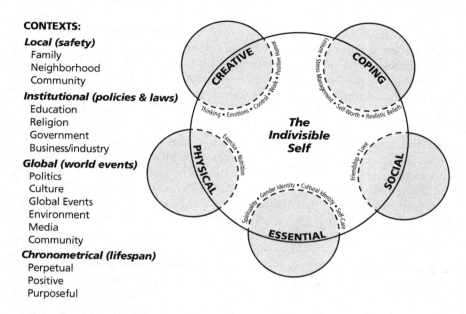

Figure 3.1 The indivisible self model of wellness (IS-WEL). *Note:* Creative = creative self; coping = coping self; social = social self; essential = essential self; physical = physical self. From *The Indivisible Self: An Evidence-Based Model of Wellness,* by T. J. Sweeney and J. E. Myers. Greensboro, NC: Author. Copyright 2003, 2009. Reprinted with permission.

Higher-Order Wellness Factor

At the core of the model is a single, higher order factor identified as *total wellness.* Myers (1992) defined total wellness as a quest for humanity to achieve maximum functioning that encompasses the mind, the body, and the spirit. Reflecting the holistic perspective of the model, total wellness illustrates the fact that individual components of a person's life cannot be separated out without impacting other areas. Each individual person would have his or her own version of what total wellness looks like depending on the individual's wants, needs, and desires. The measure of a person's total wellness is indicative of how well he or she is meeting life's challenges and achieving personal goals.

Five Second-Order Factors

Collectively, these five second-order factors comprise the *indivisible self.* Identified by a series of statistical analyses performed on the 17 discrete factors of wellness that had been identified by researchers in previous wellness research, each of these second-order factors represents specific components of an individual's healthy functioning that can be assessed as a viable area for counseling interventions. Furthermore, an individual's strength in one dimension can be mobilized to enhance functioning and overcome deficiencies in other dimensions. Using this approach, counselors can help their clients create positive change in their lives by focusing on strengths rather than weaknesses (Myers & Sweeney, 2004).

The first second-order factor is known as the *creative self*. It represents those attributes that allow us to make a unique place for ourselves among others in our social interactions. There are five components to this factor: thinking, emotions, control, positive humor, and work. These components collectively function to help us define our individual personality. A healthy functioning creative self enhances our capacity to live life more fully. According to Myers and Sweeney (2005), both research and clinical experience support the idea that "the ability to think clearly, perceive accurately, and respond appropriately can help decrease stress and enhance the humor response, which in turn affects the immune system positively" (p. 34).

The second factor is titled the *coping self*. The coping self reflects our manner of dealing with life's demands. It includes four components: realistic beliefs, stress management, self-worth, and leisure. These components help determine how we respond to life events and provide us with the means to overcome or look beyond the potentially negative aspects of these life events. Freeing ourselves of irrational beliefs will eliminate the source of many of the frustrations and disappointments we encounter. Likewise, the ability to engage in enjoyable leisure activities allows us to grow in creative and spiritual dimensions, further strengthening the relationship between the second-order wellness factors (Myers & Sweeney, 2005).

The third factor is the *social self*. It includes two components: friendship and love. The social self describes how we connect with others. Relationships with others provide us with additional positive sources of individual wellness. The quality of our lives is enhanced when we feel connected to and engage in intimate relationships with others. In discussing the importance of the social self, Myers and Sweeney (2005) note the extant research supporting the connection between separation (isolation) from others and a variety of poor health conditions, including a greater susceptibility to premature death.

The fourth factor is the *essential self*. The essential self incorporates our sense of meaning, purpose, and hopefulness toward life. It is comprised of four components: spirituality, self-care, gender identity, and cultural identity. Our spiritual beliefs and convictions, gender identity, and cultural identity all serve as filters through which our life experiences are viewed. They also reflect how others view and respond to us. Self-care, according to Myers and Sweeney (2005), includes those "proactive efforts to live long and well" (p. 35).

The final second-order factor is the *physical self.* The physical self is comprised of two components: exercise and nutrition. Although the physical components of wellness are often overemphasized in other models of wellness, they do play an integral role in holistic wellness. As Myers and Sweeney (2005) note, we feel much better about ourselves when we are physically fit. Proper diet and exercise allow us to have the strength and energy to do the things that bring us pleasure and purpose, and are fundamental to overall wellness.

Contextual Factors

Earlier it was noted that the IS-WEL model has a strong contextual component. Human functioning cannot be considered in a vacuum. Instead, a full understanding of the individual must include knowledge of his or her contextual or environmental situation and influences. The indivisible self is, therefore, both affected by and has an effect on the world around it (Myers & Sweeney, 2005). Within the IS-WEL model four contexts are defined: local, institutional, global, and chronometrical.

Local
The *local* context includes those microsystems of which we are a part: Families, neighborhoods, and communities are all examples of local contexts. These contexts help us define the world we live in and shape the way we think, feel, and act. In times of challenge and turmoil, we retreat to the familiar surroundings of our local contexts as they provide us with comfort, strength, and support.

Institutional
The *institutional* context includes the macro system institutions of education, government, religion, business, and industry. These institutional contexts have both a direct and indirect effect on our lives. Policies, laws, regulations, and institutional rules established by these various contexts all play an instrumental role in determining how we are able to achieve wellness in our lives and the means we will have available to achieve our wellness goals.

Global
Global contexts include politics, culture, global events, and the environment. They include factors that have profound effects on our lives, but are outside of our immediate control. A central concept of this context is the impact world events have on an individual's sense of personal wellness. War, famine, and economic recessions are all examples of global contexts that can impact wellness. These events change the climate in which we live and

change the importance we place on different components of our wellness. As some areas become challenged, we may seek to strengthen our wellness in other areas where we have greater freedom and control.

Chronometrical

The final context through which wellness should be examined is called *chronometrical*. It refers to the fact that individuals change over the course of time in both predictable and unpredictable ways. Developmentally there are stages that we all will progress through during the course of our lives. Our wellness represents the collective effects of all our previous choices in life. As Myers and Sweeney (2005) have noted, "Wellness choices made earlier in life have a cumulative positive effect as we grow older" (p. 36). As a result, individuals should be cognizant of the long-term, as well as short-term, implications of the decisions they make.

APPLYING THE IS-WEL MODEL IN WORKING WITH COLLEGE ATHLETES

When using the IS-WEL model in a counseling setting, counselors seek to assess where an individual's strengths lie and determine how these strengths can be mobilized to enhance functioning and overcome deficiencies in other dimensions. By focusing on strengths rather than weaknesses, counselors are better able to help clients create positive change in their lives. To identify the areas of strength for each individual student athlete, counselors could use the Five Factor Wellness Inventory (5F-Wel; Myers & Sweeney, 2005). The 5F-Wel is an empirically supported instrument designed to measure the components of wellness described in the IS-WEL model. It consists of 73 items to which participants are asked to respond to a series of behavioral and attitudinal statements (e.g., "I believe that I am a worthwhile person") using a 4-point Likert-type scale ranging from strongly agree (4) to strongly disagree (1). A raw score is obtained for each scale by adding the individual items that comprise that scale. For comparative purposes, the raw scores are then converted to a common metric using a linear transformation process. The transformed scores range in value between 25 and 100, with higher scores indicating higher levels of wellness. Based on the results of this assessment, both counselor and student can work collaboratively to establish a treatment plan aimed at improving emotional functioning and fostering positive mental health.

Aided by the multidimensional nature of the IS-WEL, counselors who choose to use this model in their work with individual athletes are provided an excellent framework for wholly addressing the heightened adjustment concerns, developmental challenges, and psychosocial stressors to which these students are particularly vulnerable (Watson & Kissinger, 2007). The following suggestions are provided to help counselors effectively work with their student-athlete clients to develop wellness plans in each of the dimensions (second-order factors) of wellness included in the IS-WEL model.

Addressing the *creative self*, counselors could focus on helping athletes identify their vocational interests outside of athletics. Given that the majority of college athletes will not secure a career as a professional athlete after college, exploring career options might be a useful endeavor. In addition to assessing the interests and aptitudes of athletes, counselors also might consider examining how the skills they are developing as part of their participation in athletic programs could translate to the world of work. The ability to function as part of a team, exhibit leadership qualities, adopt a goal orientation, and function effectively in a structured environment are all skills that transfer to the world of work. By co-creating learning opportunities with athletes, counselors can strengthen the creative self by helping promote expansion of clients' interests, skills, beliefs, values, and personal qualities (Shurts & Shoffner, 2004).

To help strengthen the *coping self* in athletes, counselors could offer support in the way of stress management. Throughout the course of their academic careers, particularly during their sports' seasons, athletes experience a great deal of stress. In addition to facing the collegiate experience with the same academic, emotional, and personal goals or concerns as other students (Ferrante, Etzel, & Lantz, 1996), athletes also must manage the rigors of athletic participation, which includes both optimizing performance and effectively managing time (Watson, 2006). Many athletes devote in excess of 20 hr per week to their sport at both practice and games or competitions (Wolverton, 2008). When coupled with the time required to attend class, study, and complete class assignments, the athlete's schedule is full. When success is demanded in both the academic and athletic arena, one may easily see how stress can become a common occurrence for athletes. To help relieve stress, support services personnel should be in place: Academic tutors and counselors should be made available to athletes to address any concerns these students might have in the classroom. Additionally, athletes could be taught to recognize the early warning signs of stress so that they can be proactive and seek help, before the burden of their stress becomes too challenging to overcome and their ability to successfully compete in the classroom and on the field is compromised.

The *essential self* is one of two areas of wellness where previous researchers (Watson & Kissinger, 2007) have found that athletes have lower levels of wellness than other students not participating in collegiate athletics. As noted earlier, the essential self describes how people view themselves through different lens depending on the groups with which they are affiliated. Although most efforts to enhance the essential self focus on how individuals view themselves through the lens of their gender and cultural identity, counselors working with athletes might consider also including athletic identity as a salient lens for these clients. According to Watson and Kissinger (2007), for the majority of college athletes, "Much of their sense of being and purpose is connected to their identification with the athlete role" (p. 159). Counselors should work to help athletes expand their perspective and see beyond their self-identification as an athlete. Specifically, counselors could work with incoming freshmen to orient them to the college experience and introduce them to all of the opportunities available to them in college apart from athletics. By expanding their self-worth outside of athletics, these students become more adept at handling stress and adversity in the future because they are able to recognize that their athletic participation is only a part of who they are as a person: Shortcomings on the playing field do not mean that person is a wholly deficient individual. Working in the essential self domain also is important for athletes who may have suffered a debilitating injury or are nearing the end of their athletic eligibility.

The *social self* is another area in which athletes have been shown to have a less well perspective than other students (Watson & Kissinger, 2007). According to the IS-WEL model, the social self is strengthened when individuals feel connected to family and friends. For athletes the sense of connectedness they feel may be limited to those who are in similar situations such as theirs. Whether it be similar schedules or a like-minded understanding of what it is like to be an athlete, many athletes associate with others who are engaged in athletics: This could be teammates or athletes competing on other teams. Additionally, a negative perception of athletes may exist on some campuses as these students are seen as pampered and privileged and operating under their own set of rules (Ferrante et al., 1996; Simons, Bosworth, Fujita, & Jensen, 2007). Such negative perceptions only heighten the sense of isolation that athletes face. To help expand the social network of athletes, Valentine and Taub (1999) have suggested that athletes be encouraged to develop friendships or study partnerships with classmates, choose a roommate who is not a fellow student athlete, or participate in Greek life. These activities help to foster a sense of campus connectedness for the athlete.

In working with college athletes, it would seem that the *physical self* would not be an area counselors would need to address. However, it is an area where problems can arise that may not manifest until later in life. While most athletes are diligent in their training regimens, some may experiment with unhealthy choices as a result of the "win-at-all-costs" mentality that permeates the athletic community. Specifically, counselors could work with athletes to identify positive health choices in relation to exercise and diet. At one time or another, most athletes, male and female, have dealt with weight management concerns in their careers (Swoap & Murphy, 1995). With increasing pressure to make a specific weight class, appear attractive for judges, or to optimize performance, some athletes' focus on weight management becomes obsessive and eating-disordered behaviors develop. As a result, college counselors should be aware of these issues when working with athletes, and address the detrimental physical and psychological effects of eating disorders.

CONCLUSION

A common theme among college counselors is the difficulty they experience when attempting to engage athletes in counseling services (Maniar, Curry, Sommers-Flanagan, & Walsh, 2001; Watson, 2005). One reason for this common experience may be that many athletes feel uncomfortable seeking help outside of the athletic department from service providers who may not understand their special concerns, needs, and pressures, and as a result they overlook counseling services as a helpful option (Greenspan & Andersen, 1995). To address this concern, counselors who work closely with athletes should educate themselves on the unique issues and challenges inherent in managing the athlete role. Counselors who are able to do so are more likely to gain the trust of their clients and see them actively participate in the counseling process (Kissinger & Watson, 2005).

Furthermore, counselors should consult with athletic personnel prior to developing any wellness programs. According to Fletcher, Benshoff, and Richburg (2003), collaboration between university counselors and athletic department personnel is a realistic starting point for developing a system that advocates for interventions designed to assist the whole athlete. One way to strengthen the collaboration between counselors and athletic personnel is to increase awareness of the benefits of adopting a wellness lifestyle. To this end, counselors should consider facilitating annual informational sessions to help familiarize coaches and athletic department personnel with the IS-WEL holistic model of wellness and how its implementation can benefit the athlete academically, athletically, and socially. Creating administration and coaching staff buy-in to the wellness concept not only helps to *normalize* the counseling process, it also allows those key figures in the athletes' lives to more knowledgeably recognize problems that might be presenting barriers to wellness and engage counseling staff earlier in the process before greater problems develop.

QUESTIONS FOR DISCUSSION

1. What are some of the unique challenges athletes face in successfully completing their collegiate experiences that their non-athlete peers may not experience?

2. How are the challenges college athletes face in the classroom and in the competitive arena interconnected? Can their performance in one area affect performance in the other?

3. What do you see as an advantage of using a holistic model such as the IS-WEL, in working with college athletes? What do you see as a disadvantage to using the IS-WEL model with these students?

4. Describe how you would introduce the IS-WEL model and its concepts to college athletes. What would you say to these students to help them see the benefit that working on emotional and mental health may have on their athletic and academic performance?

5. After assessing a freshman athlete you note that the student scored lower in the social self-domain on the 5F-Wel. What are some interventions or activities you would use to help boost this student's wellness in the social self?

6. You have been asked to consult with members of the university soccer team. How would you incorporate elements of the IS-WEL model into your work with this team to optimize their mental health and increase their performance as a group?

REFERENCES

American College Health Association. (2012). *American College Health Association national college health assessment II: Reference group executive summary.* Retrieved from http://www.acha-ncha.org/docs/ACHA-NCHA-II-II_ReferenceGroup_ExecutiveSummary_Spring2012.pdf

American Psychological Association. (2013). *The state of mental health on college campuses: A growing crisis.* Retrieved from http://www.apa.org/about/gr/education/news/2011/college-campuses.aspx

Broughton, E., & Neyer, M. (2001). Advising and counseling student athletes. In *New Directions for Student Services, 93,* 47–53. San Francisco, CA: Jossey-Bass.

Carney, J. V. (2007). Humanistic wellness services for community mental health providers. *Journal of Humanistic Counseling, Education and Development, 46,* 154–171. http://dx.doi.org/10.1002/j.2161-1939.2007.tb00033.x

Ferrante, A. P., & Etzel, E., & Lantz, C. (1996). Counseling college student athletes: The problem, the need. In E. Etzel, A. P. Ferrante, & J. W. Pinkney (Eds.), *Counseling college student athletes: Issues and interventions.* Morgantown, WV: Fitness Information Technology.

Fletcher, T. B., Benshoff, J. M., & Richburg, M. J. (2003). A systems approach to understanding and counseling college student athletes. *Journal of College Counseling, 6*(1), 35–45. http://dx.doi.org/10.1002/j.2161-1882.2003.tb00225.x

Granello, P. F. (1999). College students' wellness as a function of social support and empathic ability. *Journal of College Counseling, 2,* 110–120. http://dx.doi.org/10.1002/j.2161-1882.1999.tb00149.x

Greenspan, M., & Anderson, M. B. (1995). Providing psychological services to student athletes: A developmental psychology model. In S. M. Murphy (Ed.), *Sports psychology interventions.* (pp. 177–191). Champaign, IL: Human Kinetics.

Hattie, J. A., Myers, J. E., & Sweeney, T. J. (2004). A factor structure of wellness: Theory, assessment, analysis, and practice. *Journal of Counseling and Development, 82,* 354–364. http://dx.doi.org/10.1002/j.1556-6678.2004.tb00321.x

Hinkle, J. S. (1994). Practitioners and cross-cultural assessment: A practical guide to information and training. *Measurement and Evaluation in Counseling and Development, 27,* 103-115.

Kissinger, D. B., & Watson, J. C. (2005). Counseling college student athletes: A working alliance model approach. *The Academic Athletic Journal, 18(1),* 42–55.

Maniar, S. D., Curry, L. A., Sommers-Flanagan, J., & Walsh, J. A. (2001). Student-athlete preferences in seeking help when confronted with sport performance problems. *The Sport Psychologist, 15,* 25–223.

Murray, M. A. (1997). The counseling needs of college student athletes. *Dissertation Abstracts International, 58,* (06), 2088A. (UMI No. 9737427)

Myers, J. E. (1992). Wellness, prevention, development: The cornerstone of the profession. *Journal of Counseling and Development, 71,* 136–139. Retrieved from http://dx.doi.org/10.1002/j.1556-6676.1992.tb02188.x

Myers, J. E., Sweeney, T. J., & Witmer, J. M. (2000). The wheel of wellness, counseling for wellness: A holistic approach to treatment planning. *Journal of Counseling and Development, 78,* 251–266.

Myers, J. E., & Sweeney, T. J. (2004). The indivisible self: An evidenced based model of wellness. *The Journal of Individual Psychology, 60,* 234–244. http://dx.doi.org/10.1002/j.1556-6678.2008.tb00536.x

Myers, J. E., & Sweeney, T. J. (2005). *Counseling for wellness: Theory, research, and practice.* Alexandria, VA: American Counseling Association.

Myers, J. E., & Sweeney, T. J. (2008). Wellness counseling: The evidence base for practice. *Journal of Counseling and Development, 86,* 482–493.

NCAA (2012). *NCAA president gives candid talk about challenges facing intercollegiate athletics.* Retrieved from http://www.odu.edu/news/2012/10/president_s_lecture__1#.VOEPVtg5Czk

Osborn, C. J. (2005). Research on college student wellness. In J. E. Myers & T. J. Sweeney (Eds.), *Counseling for wellness: Theory, research, and practice* (pp. 77–88). Alexandria, VA: American Counseling Association.

Parham, W. (1993). The intercollegiate athlete: A 1990's profile. *The Counseling Psychologist, 21,* 411–429.

Shurts, W. M., & Shoffner, M. F. (2004). Providing career counseling for collegiate student athletes: A learning theory approach. *Journal of Career Development, 31,* 95–109. http://dx.doi.org/10.1177/089484530403100202

Simons, H. D., Bosworth, C., Fujita, S., & Jensen, M. (2007). The athlete stigma in higher education. *College Student Journal, 41,* 251–273.

Swoap, R. A., & Murphy, S. M. (1995). Eating disorders and weight management in athletes. *Sport Psychology Interventions,* 307–329.

Valentine, J. J., & Taub, D. J. (1999). Responding to the developmental needs of student athletes. *Journal of College Counseling, 2,* 164–179. Retrieved from http://dx.doi.org/10.1002/j.2161-1882.1999.tb00153.x

Watson, J C. (2005). College student-athletes' attitudes toward help-seeking behavior and expectations of counseling services. *Journal of College Student Development, 46*, 442–449. Retrieved from http://dx.doi.org/10.1353/csd.2005.0044

Watson, J. C. (2006). Student athletes and counseling: Factors influencing the decision to seek counseling services. *College Student Journal, 40*(1), 35–42.

Watson, J. C., & Kissinger, D. B. (2007). Athletic participation and wellness: Implications for counseling college student athletes. *Journal of College Counseling, 10*, 153–162. Retrieved from http://dx.doi.org/10.1002/j.2161-1882.2007.tb00015.x

Witmer, J. M., & Sweeney, T. J. (1992). A holistic model for wellness and prevention over the life span. *Journal of Counseling & Development, 71*(2), 140–148.

Wolverton, B. (2008). Athletes' hours renew debate over college sports. *The Chronicle of Higher Education.* Retrieved from http://chronicle.com

CHAPTER 4

ADDING INJURY TO INSULT

Understanding College Athletes With Learning Disabilities and Concussions

Whitney Griffin

ABSTRACT

College athletes in Division I sports are at an increased risk of physical injuries. More clinical and legal interests are flourishing around invisible injuries and deficits, such as concussions, learning disabilities (LD), and attention deficit hyperactive disorder (ADHD). When internal impairments collide with external forces, athletes occupy a qualitatively unique position for physical and neuropsychological recovery. In order to understand the convergence of these impairments, LD, ADHD, and concussions are juxtaposed in the context of Division I collegiate athletics, specifically the high-collision and revenue-generating sports of football and men's basketball. Cognitive rehabilitation interventions for impaired executive functions are identified. Implications for post-concussion classroom support for college athletes with LD and/or ADHD are discussed.

Making the Connection, pages 47–61

INTRODUCTION

Attention deficit hyperactive disorder (ADHD) is the most common childhood neurobehavioral disorder, affecting between 2% and 5% of American school-aged children, with boys experiencing the disorder four to nine times more than girls (American Psychiatric Association, 2000; Lee, Oakland, Jackson, & Gutting, 2008). Little research has been conducted on the prevalence rates and course of ADHD in athletes. In a survey given to 870 interscholastic athletes, researchers found the rate of diagnosed ADHD to be 7.3%, which is higher than the prevalence rates for the general population (Heil, Hartman, Robinson, & Teegarden, 2002). In the same study, the distribution of ADHD also tended to vary by sport, with the highest levels seen in football (17.5%). ADHD thus appears to be more prevalent in athletes than in the general population (Escalona, Esfandiari, Broshek, & Freeman, 2010), perhaps owing to a tendency for those with ADHD to be drawn to physical activity (Burton, 2000), especially fast-paced and stimulating activities (Barkley, 1998). Because individuals with ADHD are often prone to an impulsive style of play, it is hypothesized that they are more at risk for concussion (Escalona et al., 2010). Theoretically, those with untreated ADHD are likely to thrive in sports or positions that benefit from spontaneous or unpredictable behavior (e.g., a running back in football) and more likely to struggle in positions that require disciplined focus (e.g., a defensive player that needs to stay in a certain physical zone) (Escalona et al.). Male football players, especially those in positions that benefit from spontaneous behavior, are therefore an at-risk subpopulation warranting further investigation.

A second neurocognitive concern for athletes is learning disabilities (LD), a term used to describe a constellation of disorders manifested by significant difficulties in reading, mathematics, writing, and/or processing skills that can occur alone or in varying combinations ranging in severity (Escalona et al., 2010). Common LD include, but are not limited to, dyslexia (impaired accuracy and/or rate of oral reading of real words and written spelling), dyscalculia (impaired counting, math fact retrieval, and calculation), dysgraphia (impaired handwriting), nonverbal learning disability (impaired social cognition, visual-spatial organization, and/or complex motor skills), and oral and written language disability (impaired word retrieval, listening and reading comprehension, and/or oral and written expression) (Berninger & Miller, 2011). Although LD cannot be cured, the underlying conditions can be managed so that those with LD can adapt to their environment (Shapiro & Gallico, 1993). It is estimated that 2.7% of the total population of athletes has a diagnosed LD (N4A Committee on Learning Disabilities, 1998). It is also argued that athletes with the added hurdle of managing a LD face a range of unique challenges that result in a qualitatively different educational experience than that experienced by non athletes (Etzel, Ferrante, & Pinkney, 1996), and even by athletes without LD (Bowen & Levin, 2003).

Why does this matter? College athletes with LD are sometimes exploited because of their athletic prowess (Sedlacek & Adams-Gaston, 1992) and often achieve more success in the athletic arena than in the classroom (Broshek & Freeman, 2005). They can be recruited to a university despite the lack of adequate preparation to deal with the academic challenge (Escalona et al., 2010). Adding insult to injury, it appears that having LD might have greater consequences for athletes who experience multiple concussions. A study by Collins and colleagues (1999) found that athletes who had LD and experienced multiple concussions performed significantly worse on problem solving and information processing tests than players with multiple concussions who had no history of LD.

The existing literature establishes the overlapping barriers that college athletes face with LD, ADHD, and/or concussions. The need to systematically protect collegiate athletes from re-injuring themselves and from returning to play prematurely is becoming more heightened (Lovell & Collins, 1998) as more athletes continue to commit homicide and suicide as a result of functional brain damage. With this in mind, the purpose of this chapter is to bring awareness to stakeholders in the affairs of athletics and the broader academic community about invisible impairments that leave real impacts in the lives of Division I athletes. Research on LD, ADHD, and sports concussions have become distinct and growing areas of interest in the last decade. In the sections that follow, my goal is to synthesize and apply the existing knowledge and literature to a marginalized yet exploited group of collegiate athletes: those with LD and/or ADHD who may also suffer a sports concussion. Although these different stressors in an athlete's life impact the development of their identity, academic performance, mental health, and physical well-being, these students often continue to play high-impact sports. After juxtaposing LD, ADHD, and concussions, evidence-based cognitive rehabilitation interventions for impaired executive functions are identified. Finally, implications for post-concussion academic support for athletes with LD and/or ADHD are discussed to inform decision-making practices at Division I institutions. Practitioners are encouraged to match similar experiences with existing research to implement and modify practical interventions for athletes with these comorbid factors in order to foster students' intellectual identities.

LEARNING DISABILITIES, ADHD, AND EXECUTIVE FUNCTION DEFICITS

The inability to provide an agreed upon definition of a learning disability has been a handicap that has caused confusion and misdiagnoses in research and practice. To address the limitations of previous definitions while taking a neuropsychological approach, Mapou (2009) provides a comprehensive definition of a learning disability for adults:

> A learning disability is a neurodevelopmental disorder affecting a specific academic and/or cognitive skill that occurs in the presence of intact skills in most other realms...since birth. Although most learning disabilities affect academic skills...a learning disability can also affect specific areas of neuropsychological functioning, including attention, executive functions and problem-solving abilities, spoken language, visuospatial skills, or learning and memory. A learning disability substantially limits functioning in one or more aspects of a person's life (e.g., school, work, home, social). (p. 8)

ADHD affects at least 5% of adults in the United States (Barkley, Murphy, & Fisher, 2008) and may affect 2% to 4% of the college student population (DuPaul et al., 2001). The three most common subtypes of ADHD that are used for diagnostic criteria are inattention or distractibility, hyperactivity, and impulsivity (Batshaw, Pellegrino, & Roizen, 2008). There are also reports on core deficits in measures of attention, information processing speed, executive functioning, learning, and memory (Barkley, Murphy, O'Connell, Anderson, Connor, 2006). Woods, Lovejoy, Stutts, Ball, and Fals-Steward (2002) found deficits in information processing speed, divided and sustained attention, cognitive flexibility, impulsivity, organization, planning, auditory-verbal list learning, and timed word generation. According to the *Diagnostic and Statistical Manual of Mental Disorders* (American Psychiatric Association, 2000), symptoms must occur in at least two settings (e.g., at work, home, and/or school).

Because existing definitions lack specificity, diagnosing LD or ADHD in young adulthood leads to two predictable outcomes: first, the diagnostic criteria will become less valid with age; and second, many of those who have the disorder as children will appear to have outgrown the disorder by adulthood, whereas in fact they have only outgrown the criteria (Barkley, 2010). A major obstacle to retrospective diagnosis is that it is significantly biased by current functioning (McGough & Barkley, 2004). This may prevent eligible young adults in college from receiving necessary help if clinicians are unable to find a history of symptoms in childhood or lack reliable third-party corroboration. Furthermore, because research on ADHD is newer in adults than in children, it may be unrecognized in college students, who are at risk for low academic achievement and other related problems (Weyandt et al., 2003).

ADHD was first defined by impairment in attention, but recent literature has suggested that these problems may stem from executive function impairments (Mapou, 2009). Executive functions are actually a system of high-level cognitive processes in the frontal lobe that manage and regulate other cognitive processes, such as planning, organization, time management, working memory, and metacognition. Working memory is the ability to hold information in mind while performing complex tasks. Metacognition is the ability to stand back and take a bird's-eye view of oneself in a situation. Executive skills allow us to organize our behavior over time, override immediate demands in favor of longer-term goals, plan and organize activities, sustain attention, and persist to complete a task (Dawson & Guare, 2004). Additionally, executive skills are crucial to regulating or monitoring our emotions and thoughts, in order to work more efficiently and effectively. If just one of these skills is missing, the system is incomplete.

The impact of ADHD on adult life is substantial. In a longitudinal study of children with ADHD into adulthood, adults with ADHD had significantly fewer years of education, a lower GPA, a lower class ranking in their last year of high school, more symptoms of ADHD at work, a lower job-performance rating from their employer, and more arrests (Barkley, Fischer, Smallish & Fletcher, 2002). Research also reports that adults with ADHD show deficits in socio-emotional competence (Friedman et al., 2003) and considerable co-occurrence of ADHD with mood, anxiety, personality, and substance use disorders (Barkley, 2006). It is estimated that 25% of students with ADHD have a co-occurring learning disability (Kotkin, Forness, & Kavale, 2001). In a large community-based study of over 3,000 adults, Kessler et al. (2006) found that more than 80% of adults with ADHD had at least one co-occurring psychiatric disorder. In comparison with children, the use of multiple medications in adults with ADHD was more likely to be necessary because of co-occurring disorders (Barkley Murphy & Fisher, 2008).

Race and socioeconomic status are not impervious to ADHD, although there are no causal relationships. Reid et al. (1998) reported that African American children are more likely to be exposed to prenatal risk factors, psychosocial stressors, and economic disadvantage, which in turn adversely affect ADHD behaviors. In a study on possible racial differences in ADHD symptoms in college freshmen, Lee, Oakland, Jackson, and Gutting (2008) found that the rates of African American students who reported symptom totals beyond DSM-IV-TR thresholds exceed that for Caucasian students on all three subtypes of ADHD. However, the researchers admit that little support has been found for whether racial differences are due to actual behavioral differences, the use of invalid scales with culturally different children, a negative halo effect, or other psychological qualities. The correlations between Black Americans seem to dance around socially constructed issues of race, class, and gender. For further discussion of this topic, see the book *White Prescriptions?: The Dangerous Social Potential for Ritalin and other Psychotropic Drugs to Harm Black Boys* (Fitzgerald, 2009).

In a study on self-medication for ADHD, college students grappled with the pursuit of a coherent sense of self when balancing their "authentic" identity and "medicated" identity (Loe & Cuttino, 2008). To manage this conflict, many students accepted and rationalized situational medical control while employing strategies designed to emphasize agency and preserve a sense of authentic selfhood. In this context, strategic pharmaceutical use became a way to occupy a middle ground between medical optimization and authenticity (Loe & Cuttino, 2008). Giving up the perceived "authentic" identity would mean permanently being controlled by medicine that blots out unique personalities. Conversely, giving up the "medicated" identity would mean losing the ability to manage performance and achievement, as defined by executive functions. Thus, the social construction of ADHD is a non-medical aspect that further marginalizes students with the stigma of having a learning disability.

As defined above, LD and ADHD in adults are developmental disorders. A history of a learning disability or ADHD is common in adults with a history of traumatic brain injury. This is because adults with ADHD or learning disabilities, who experience low self-esteem and/or associated impulsivity, can be risk takers and can act without thinking about the consequences of their actions; this increases their risk for brain injury (Mapou, 2009). Distinguishing between the effects of a brain injury and those of ADHD can sometimes be difficult because both affect attention, executive functioning, learning, and working memory. These confounding effects are further complicated in athletes with learning disabilities or ADHD who also play high-impact sports.

MILD TRAUMATIC BRAIN INJURIES (mTBI)

Concussion is a subset of mild traumatic brain injury (mTBI), which is at the less-severe end of the brain injury spectrum (Harmon et al., 2013). The Fourth International Conference on Concussion in Sport held in Zurich in 2012 defined concussions as a complex pathophysiological process affecting the brain, induced by biomechanical forces, and that may be caused either by a direct blow to the head, face, neck or elsewhere on the body with an "impulsive" force transmitted to the head (McCrory et al., 2013). Thus, concussions induce metabolic and functional disturbances rather than structural damage (Ptito, Chen, & Johnston, 2007; Sady, Vaughan, & Gioia, 2011). It is estimated that as many as 3.8 million concussions occur in the United States every year during competitive sports and recreational activities; however, as many as 50% of the concussions may go unreported (Harmon). Even though it is the most recognizable sign, not all concussions cause a loss of consciousness. In fact, only 8.9% of the 1,003 reported injuries involved loss of consciousness, and only 27.7% involved amnesia after a second concussion (Guskiewicz, Weaver, Padua, & Garrett, 2000).

Failing to self-report concussions or minimizing symptoms are both extremely dangerous and common. In a confidential survey of more than 1,500 high-school football players' concussion histories, researchers noted that more than 40% believed that they were concussed but deliberately did not reveal this information for fear of losing playing time (McCrea, Hammeke, Olsen, Leo, & Guskiewicz, 2004).

A variety of somatic and cognitive symptoms are spontaneously reported during concussion assessment. These symptoms or problems often include headache, dizziness, photophobia, memory, concentration, and fogginess. (Iverson, Gaetz, Lovell, & Collins, 2004). It is considered standard practice that an athlete's neurocognitive performance must return to baseline or better before returning to play (Moser, 2007). Two available assessments are the traditional Post-Concussion Symptom Scale (Lovell et al., 2006) and the computerized Immediate Post-Concussion Assessment and Cognitive Testing (ImPACT) battery.

Once concussed, an athlete is at a statistically increased risk for recurrent concussions (Slobounov et al., 2010). Previously concussed athletes are four to six times more likely to experience a second concussion, even if the second blow is relatively mild (Guskiewicz et al., 2003). Perhaps the most dangerous risk of sustaining a first concussion is second impact syndrome, which occurs when an athlete who sustains a head injury—often a concussion or worse injury, such as a cerebral contusion—sustains a second head injury before symptoms associated with the first have cleared (Cantu, 1998). After a notorious demonstration of second impact syndrome that left an eighth-grade football player paralyzed, Washington state passed the Lystedt Law in 2009 that requires all athletes under the age of 18 who are suspected of having sustained a concussion to be removed from practice or a game and not allowed to return until cleared by a medical professional. The law also requires athletes, parents, and coaches to be educated each year about the dangers of concussions.

In post-concussion syndrome, recovery is prolonged and the afflicted individual continues to experience persistent symptoms, such as: (a) difficulties in attention, concentration, and/or speed of mental processing; (b) emotional symptoms of irritability, clinical depression, or moodiness; and (c) physical symptoms of headaches, fatigue, and/or sleep difficulties (Guskiewicz et al., 2007; Kontos, Covassin, Elbin, & Parker, 2012; Moser, 2007). Recovery from concussion varies by individual and severity of concussion and management should be taken on a case-by-case basis (Escalona et al., 2010). Persistent post-concussion syndrome can manifest in problems at school with specific difficulties, such as mental slowness in completing assignments, problems understanding verbal communication in group discussions, greater distractibility and poor concentration, ineffective multitasking, and severe fatigue (Moser, 2007). Higher-level executive functions are affected, such as shifting attention (cognitive and behavioral flexibility), dual-task processing, and divided attention (Mateer, Kerns & Eso, 1996). The effects of mTBI on executive function are dynamic in the sense that these abilities are impaired immediately after injury and recover at a variable rate depending on the severity of focal and diffuse effects (Cicerone, Levin, Malec, Stuss, & Whyte, 2006). There is also evidence that athletes with multiple concussions could have a lingering deficit in memory (Iverson, Echemendia, Lamarre, Brooks, & Gaetz, 2012).

Because concussions cannot be "seen," family, friends, teachers, and peers often expect concussed individuals to fully recover and "shake it off" (Moser, 2007). Yet, long after the injury, academic performance may greatly suffer and may be misinterpreted as laziness or attitudinal or behavioral procrastination. These performance issues can be injurious to athletes when misinterpreted by professors and coaches, especially if post-concussion syndrome is undiagnosed. The decline in cognitive performance can lead to further stigmatization of academic capabilities for college athletes.

Premorbid LD and/or ADHD are risk factors for concussion recovery and little research has examined the effect of these conditions on academic outcomes for athletes. College athletes with LD who experienced concussions may have had less brain reserve capacity than those without LD (Collins et al., 1999). The margin of cognitive reserve may be less in athletes with LD and the threshold for manifesting neurobehavioral morbidity may be lower. LD can also make the initial diagnosis of concussion more complex and confusing. Finally, athletes with LD may have difficulty learning the proper techniques for safe play or could have neurobehavioral characteristics (e.g., impulsivity and attentional impairment) leading to increased risk of injury (Collins et al., 1999). With this knowledge, it is important for support service personnel to monitor athletes before they enter their first practice to obtain baseline academic and physical performances.

IMPLICATIONS: CLASSROOM SUPPORTS AFTER CONCUSSIONS

Students with learning disabilities have a propensity to become involved in athletics. In a narrative of adults with dyslexia, McNulty (2003) found that adults with dyslexia drew a sense of self-esteem from success in athletics and relied on sports to connect with other children in middle school. One adult noted the role athletics played in his life as a child: "But in swimming, I excelled.... So then, all of a sudden, I was getting positive feedback, and it was very helpful to me as a kid growing up" (McNulty, p. 373). Perhaps athletics serves as a refuge for students who suffer LD trauma and low self-esteem.

Athletics provides a sphere for identity development as a leader, a team-mate, and an individual who can see ability as malleable instead of prede-termined. As much as athletics can be a niche for students with LD and/or ADHD, it is incumbent upon all support staff to create a safe zone for these college athletes to foster their intellectual identity.

Parker and Boutelle (2009) suggested executive function coaching for college students with LD and ADHD would enhance their academic success. Coaching, in contrast to traditional campus services, focused primarily on supporting students' emerging autonomy, helping them develop and man-age their executive function skills, and promoting their self-efficacy and confidence. Overall, students in the study described coaching as a person-alized, self-directed service that promoted their self-determination. They found it to be highly personalized because their coaches quickly developed an accurate understanding of how they achieved goals. Students also de-scribed coaching as a personalized service because their coaches encour-aged thoughtful risk taking through experimentation with new strategies. In comparison to other forms of assistance, students characterized coaches' mind-set as nonjudgmental, realistic about their needs, but unwaveringly positive about their potential.

Other interventions may seek to train compensatory strategies for over-coming executive-function impairments (e.g., cuing or reminding devices) where meaningful change is not made in the executive processes them-selves, but may predict improvement in tasks that were secondarily com-promised by the executive impairment (Cicerone, Levin, Malec, Stuss, & Whyte, 2006). Whether from LD or ADHD deficits, during concussion re-covery, or both, athletes would not have to rely on internal impaired ex-ecutive functions, but rather could develop habits for setting external re-minders and compensations. Learning specialists and tutors are in prime positions to be an executive function coach, since athletes must frequently interact with athletic coaches. In this way, coaching strategies that tap into superior athletic performance can be transferrable to constructing success-ful academic performances.

Individual learning styles for students with ADHD can be identified us-ing the Dunn and Dunn Learning Styles approach while concentrating on new and difficult academic knowledge or skills. Some elements include im-mediate instructional environment (e.g., bright versus soft lighting), own emotionality (e.g., motivation, preference for structure versus choice), sociological preference for learning (e.g., alone versus with peers), and physiological characteristics (e.g., time-of-day energy levels, snacking while concentrating) (Brand, Dunn, & Greb, 2002). Similarly, Dawson & Guare (2004) describe coaching and intervention strategies to enhance executive skills both at the level of the environment (e.g., changing the physical or social environment, changing the nature of the task, or changing the way cues are provided) and changing the way teachers interact with students. This literature establishes that students with LD and/or ADHD require educational techniques that are both tailored to their individual learning styles while taking into consideration their unique impairments. Using the Dunn and Dunn Learning Styles model, athletes could potentially explore their own strengths instead of harping on their inadequacies in order to take control and agency over their learning styles. Other learning style indexes are available online for free (Felder & Soloman, n.d.). Learning specialists and tutors could use these tools to create a positive feedback loop for the athlete and develop their strengths rather than only address their symptoms.

There are several approaches to the rehabilitation of students with attention and memory disorders following mTBI. One intervention for problem-solving deficits is to reduce the complexity of a multistage problem by breaking it down into manageable subgoals (Von Cramon, Matthes-Von Cramon, & Mai, 1991). Goal Management Training (GMT) is an interactive executive functioning intervention that draws upon theories concerning goal processing and sustained attention (Levine et al., 2000). In this rehabilitation protocol, individuals are taught to identity specific goals, to organize those goals into sensible, more simplistic subgoals, to keep the subgoals in mind while carrying out the respective tasks, and to stay on task while avoiding distractions (Winocur et al., 2000). Training to evaluate the current problem state (What am I doing?) is followed by specification of the relevant goals (main task), and partitioning of the problem-solving process into subgoals (steps). Students should then be assisted with the learning and retention of goals and subgoals (Do I know the steps?) and finally taught to self-monitor the results of their actions with the intended goal state (Am I doing what I planned to do?) (Cicerone, Levin, Malec, Stuss, & Whyte, 2006). In a meta-analysis of rehabilitation after a brain injury, Park and Ingles (2001) found that the few studies that attempted to rehabilitate specific skills requiring attention showed statistically significant improvements after training. Acquired deficits of attention are, in fact, treatable using specific-skills training.

The cognitive symptoms that are often experienced after a concussion create substantial roadblocks to recovery. As if post-concussive symptoms were not enough, it is hypothesized that students who engage in cognitive activity (e.g., attending class, reading, studying) stress the already under-energized brain, resulting in worsening of symptoms and potentially prolonged recovery (Majerske et al., 2008), a phenomenon known as cognitive exertion or cognitive overexertion (Sady, Vaughan, & Gioia, 2011). The therapeutic goal during concussion recovery is to find an appropriate level of cognitive exertion that does not exacerbate symptoms or cause the re-emergence of previously resolved symptoms (Valovich McLeod & Gioia,

2010). This would require efficient collaboration between medical and academic support staff since athletes still have to meet the scholarly demands of a Division-I university.

This bidirectional conversation is rare in concussion, ADHD and LD literature. These interventions can potentially be adapted and shared with the learning specialists, tutors, and sports psychologists, who provide academic support for at-risk athletes, as well as coaches, who serve as a different type of teacher. Students with LD might continue to benefit from traditional remedial education in various academic skills, but it appears that the students with mTBI might benefit from cognitive rehabilitation in such areas as memory, attention, and problem solving that could lessen the impact of the dysfunction (Beers, Goldstein, & Katz, 1994; Mateer, Kerns, & Eso, 1996). The increase of ADHD diagnoses demands that health-care practitioners understand the implications and effects of these disabilities on neuropsychological tests utilized in concussion assessment (Hunt, Mc-Camey, & Beisner, 2010). Because no two concussions are the same, there is not a one-size-fits-all approach (Sady, Vaughan, & Gioia, 2011), but there should be a team assembled with clearly defined roles. Each effective management plan must involve injured students and a carefully coordinated team of school personnel. While each institution independently determines concussion management, the information outlined in this chapter may help inform student affairs practices and communication protocols surrounding this subset of college athletes.

QUESTIONS FOR DISCUSSION

1. How would you create a profile of a student who has executive function deficits but does not have ADHD or LD?
2. If the clinicians who interpret neuropsychological test results do not yet understand college athletes with LD, should athletes with LD use the same baseline neuropsychological test as those without LD?
3. Should athletes taking medication for diagnosed ADHD stay medicated on game day?
4. Who should be held accountable when an athlete has clearly suffered a concussion but is sent back into the game a few plays later?
5. Does a coach's authority override the pressures of athletes to self-report concussive symptoms?
6. If an athletic trainer feels pressured by the coach to determine if an athlete is ready for return to play, how does this affect their ability to do their job?

REFERENCES

American Psychiatric Association. (2000). *Diagnostic and statistical manual of mental disorder* (4th ed., text revision). Washington, DC: American Psychiatric Association.

Barkley, R. (1998). *Attention-deficit hyperactivity disorder: A handbook for diagnosis and treatment* (2nd ed.). New York, NY: Guilford.

Barkley, R. (2006). *Attention deficit hyperactivity disorder: A handbook for diagnosis and treatment* (3rd ed). New York, NY: Guilford.

Barkley, R. (2010). Against the status quo: Revising the diagnostic criteria for ADHD [Letter to the editor]. *Journal of the American Academy of Child & Adolescent Psychiatry, 49,* 205–207. doi:10.1016/j.jaac.2009.12.005

Barkley, R., Fischer, M., Smallish, L., & Fletcher, K. (2002). The persistence of attention deficit hyperactivity disorder into young adulthood as a function of reporting source and definition of disorder. *Journal of Abnormal Psychology, 111,* 279–289.

Barkley, R., Murphy, K., & Fisher, M. (2008). *ADHD in adults: What the science says.* New York, NY: Guilford.

Barkley, R., Murphy, K., O'Connell, T., Anderson, D., & Connor, D. (2006). Effects of two doses of alcohol on simulator driving performance in adults with attention deficit hyperactivity disorder. *Neuropsychology, 20,* 77–87.

Batshaw, M. L., Pellegrino, L., & Roizen, N. J. (Eds.). (2008). *Children with disabilities.* Princeton, NJ: Paul H. Brookes.

Beers, S. R., Goldstein, G., & Katz, L. J. (1994). Neuropsychological differences between college students with learning disabilities and those with mild head injury. *Journal of Learning Disabilities, 27,* 315–324.

Berninger, V. W., & Miller, B. (2011). Adolescent specific learning disabilities. In B. B. Brown & M. J. Prinstein (Eds.), *Encyclopedia of Adolescence* (Vol. 3., pp. 21–29). San Diego, CA: Academic Press.

Bowen, W. G., & Levin, S. A. (2003). *Reclaiming the game: College sports and educational values.* Princeton, NJ: Princeton University Press.

Brand, S., Dunn, R., & Greb, F. (2002). Styles of students with attention deficit hyperactive disorder: Who are they and how can we teach them? *The Clearing House, 75,* 268–273.

Broshek, D. K., & Freeman, J. R. (2005). Psychiatric and neuropsychological issues in sports medicine. *Clinics in Sports Medicine, 24,* 663–679.

Burton, R. W. (2000). Mental illness in athletes. In D. Begel & R. W. Burton (Eds.), *Sport psychiatry: Theory and practice* (pp. 61–81). New York, NY: W. W. Norton.

Cantu, R. C. (1998). Second-impact syndrome. *Clinical Sports Medicine, 17*(1), 37–44.

Cicerone, K., Levin, H., Malec, J., Stuss, D., & Whyte, J. (2006). Cognitive rehabilitation interventions for executive function: Moving from bench to bedside in patients with traumatic brain injury. *Journal of Cognitive Neuroscience, 18,* 1212–1222.

Collins, M. W., Grindel, S. H., Lovell, M. R., Dede, D. E., Moser, D. J., Phalin, B. R., Nogle, S., et al. (1999). Relationship between concussion and neuropsychological performance in college football players. *Journal of the American Medical Association, 282,* 964–970.

Dawson, P., & Guare, R. (2004). *Executive skills in children and adolescents: A practical guide to assessment and intervention.* New York, NY: Guilford.

DuPaul, G. J., Schaughency, E. A., Weyandt, L. L., Tripp, G., Kiesner, J., Ota, K., & Stanish, H. (2001). Self-report of ADHD symptoms in university students: Cross-gender and cross-national prevalence. *Journal of Learning Disabilities, 34,* 370–379.

Escalona, A., Esfandiari, A., Broshek, D., & Freeman, J. (2010). Counseling athletes within the context of neurocognitive concerns. In F. Webbe (Ed.), *The hand-book of sport neuropsychology.* New York, NY: Springer.

Etzel, E. F., Ferrante, A. P., & Pinkney, J. W. (1996). *Counseling college student athletes: Issues and interventions* (2nd ed). Morgantown, WV: Fitness Information Technology.

Felder, R., & Soloman, B. (n.d.). *Learning styles and strategies.* Retrieved from http://www4.ncsu.edu/unity/lockers/users/f/felder/public/ILSdir/styles.htm

Fitzgerald, T. (2009). *White prescriptions? The dangerous social potential for Ritalin and other psychotropic drugs to harm Black boys.* Boulder, CO: Paradigm.

Friedman, S., Rapport, L., Lumley, M., Tzelepis, A., Van Voorhis, A., Stettner, L., & Kakaati, L. (2003). Aspects of social and emotional competence in adults with attention deficit hyperactivity disorder. *Neuropsychology, 17,* 50–58.

Guskiewicz, K. M., Marshall, S. W., Bailes, J., McCrea, M., Harding, H. P., Matthews, A., Mihalik, J. R., et al. (2007). Recurrent concussion and risk of depression in retired professional football players. *Medicine and Science in Sports and Exercise, 39,* 903–909.

Guskiewicz, K. M., McCrea, M., Marshall, S. W., Cantu, R. C., Randolph, C., Barr, W., Onate, J., & Kelly, J. (2003). Cumulative effects associated with recurrent concussion in collegiate football players: The NCAA concussion study. *Journal of the American Medical Association, 290,* 2549–2555.

Guskiewicz, K. M., Weaver, N. L., Padua, D. A., & Garrett, W. E., Jr. (2000). Epidemiology of concussion in collegiate and high-school football players. *American Journal of Sports Medicine, 28,* 643–650.

Harmon, K., Drezner, J., Gammons, M., Guskiewicz, K., Halstead, M., Herring, S., & Roberts, W. (2013). American Medical Society for Sports Medicine position statement: Concussion in sport. *British Journal of Sports Medicine, 47,* 15–26. doi:10.1136/bjsports-2012-091941

Heil, J., Hartman, D., Robinson, G., & Teegarden, L. (2002). *Attention deficit hyperactivity disorder in athletes.* Retrieved from http://coaching.usolympicteam.com/coaching/kpub.nsf/v/adhd

Hunt, T., McCamey, K., & Beisner, A. (2010). The relationship between ADHD and concussion history on neuropsychological test scores in collegiate athletes. *Medicine & Science in Sports & Exercise, 42,* 114. doi: 10.1249/01. MSS.0000386000.82770.27

Iverson, G. L., Echemendia, R. J., Lamarre, A. K., Brooks, B. L., & Gaetz, M. B. (2012). Possible lingering effects of multiple past concussions. *Rehabilitation Research and Practice,* (316575), 1–7.

Iverson, G. L., Gaetz, M., Lovell, M. R., & Collins, M. W. (2004). Relation between subjective fogginess and neuropsychological testing following concussion. *Journal of the International Neuropsychological Society, 10,* 904–906.

Kessler, R., Adler, L., Barkley, R., Biederman, J., Conners, C., Demler, O., Faraone, S., et al. (2006). The prevalence and correlates of adult ADHD in the United States: Results from the national comorbidity survey replication. *The American Journal of Psychiatry, 163,* 716–723.

Kontos, A. P., Covassin, T., Elbin, R. J., & Parker, T. (2012). Depression and neurocognitive performance after concussion among male and female high school and collegiate athletes. *Archives of Physical Medicine and Rehabilitation, 93,* 1751–1756.

Kotkin, R. A., Forness, S. R., & Kavale, K. A. (2001). Comorbid ADHD and LD: Diagnosis, special education, and intervention. In D. Hallahan & B. K. Keogh (Eds.), *Research and global perspectives in learning disabilities* (pp. 43–64). Mahmah, N.J.: Erlbaum.

Lee, D., Oakland, T., Jackson, G., & Glutting, J. (2008). Estimated prevalence of attention deficit hyperactivity disorder symptoms among college freshmen. *Journal of Learning Disabilities, 41,* 371–384.

Levine, B., Robertson, I. H., Clare, L., Carter, G., Hong, J., Wilson, B. A., Duncan, J., & Stuss, D. T. (2000). Rehabilitation of executive functioning: An experimental-clinical validation of goal management training. *Journal of the International Neuropsychological Society 6,* 299–312.

Loe, M., & Cuttino, L. (2008). Grappling with the medicated self: The case of ADHD in college students. *Symbolic Interaction, 31,* 303–323.

Lovell, M. R., & Collins, M. W. (1998). Neuropsychological assessment of the college football player. *The Journal of Head Trauma Rehabilitation, 13,* 9–26.

Lovell, M. R., Iverson, G. L., Collins, M. W., Podell, K., Johnston, K. M., Pardini, D., Pardini, J., Norwig, J., & Maroon, J. C. (2006). Measurement of symptoms following sports-related concussion: Reliability and normative data for the post-concussion scale. *Applied Neuropsychology, 13,* 166–174.

Majerske, C. W., Mihalik, J. P., Ren, D., Collins, M. W., Reddy, C. C., Lovell, M. R., & Wagner, A. K. (2008). Concussion in sports: Postconcussive activity levels, symptoms, and neurocognitive performance. *Journal of Athletic Training, 43,* 265–274. doi:10.4085/1062-6050-43.3.265

Mapou, R. L., & American Academy of Clinical Neuropsychology. (2009). *Adult learning disabilities and ADHD: Research-informed assessment.* Oxford, England: Oxford University Press.

Mateer, C., Kerns, K., & Eso, K. (1996). Management of attention and memory disorders following traumatic brain injury. *Journal of Learning Disabilities, 29,* 618–632.

McCrea, M., Hammeke, T., Olsen, G., Leo, P., & Guskiewicz, K. (2004). Unreported concussion in high-school football players: Implications for prevention. *Clinical Journal of Sport Medicine, 14,* 13–17.

McCrory, P., Meeuwisse, W. H., Aubry, M., Cantu, B., Dvořák, J., Echemendia, R. J., & Turner, M. (2013). Consensus statement on concussion in sport: The Fourth International Conference on Concussion in Sport held in Zurich, November 2012. *British Journal of Sports Medicine, 47,* 250–258. doi:10.1136/bjsports-2013-092313

McGough, J., & Barkley, R. A. (2004). Diagnostic controversies in adult attention deficit hyperactivity disorder. *The American Journal of Psychiatry, 161,* 1948–1956.

McNulty, M. (2003). Dyslexia and the life course. *Journal of Learning Disabilities 36,* 363–381.

Moser, R. S. (2007). The growing public concern of sports concussion: The new psychology practice frontier. *Professional Psychology: Research and Practice, 38,* 699–704.

N4A Committee on Learning Disabilities. (1998). *Services for student athletes with learning disabilities. Survey results May 1998.* Retrieved from http://www.nfoura.org/ Committees/Cold/surveymay99.html

Park, N. W., & Ingles, J. L. (2001). Effectiveness of attention rehabilitation after an acquired brain injury: A meta-analysis. *Neuropsychology, 15*(2), 199–210. doi:10.1037//0894-4105.15.2.199

Parker, D., & Boutelle, K. (2009). Executive function coaching for college students with learning disabilities and ADHD: A new approach for fostering self-development. *Learning Disabilities Research & Practice, 24,* 204–215.

Ptito, A., Chen, J.-K., & Johnston, K. M. (2007). Contributions of functional magnetic resonance imaging (fMRI) to sport concussion evaluation. *Neuro-Rehabilitation, 22,* 217–27. Retrieved from http://www.ncbi.nlm.nih.gov/ pubmed/17917172

Reid, R., DuPaul, G. J., Power, T. J., Anastopoulos, A.D., Rogers-Adkinson, D., Noll, M., & Riccio, C. (1998). Assessing culturally different students for attention deficit hyperactivity disorder using behavior rating scales. *Journal of Abnormal Child Psychology, 26,* 187–198.

Sady, M. D., Vaughan, C. G., & Gioia, G. A. (2011). School and the concussed youth: recommendations for concussion education and management. *Physical Medicine and Rehabilitation Clinics of North America, 22,* 701–719.

Sedlacek, W. E., & Adams-Gason, J. (1992). Predicting the academic success of student athletes using SAT and non-cognitive variables. *Journal of Counseling and Development, 70,* 724–727.

Shapiro, B. K., & Gallico, R. P. (1993). Learning disabilities. *Pediatric Clinics of North America, 40,* 491–505.

Slobounov, S. M., Zhang, K., Pennell, D., Ray, W., Johnson, B., & Sebastianelli, W. (2010). Functional abnormalities in normally appearing athletes following mild traumatic brain injury: A functional MRI study. *Experimental Brain Research, 202,* 341–354.

Valovich McLeod T., & Gioia G. (2010). Cognitive rest: The often neglected aspect of concussion management. *Athletic Therapy Today, 15,* 1–3.

Von Cramon, D., Matthes-von Cramon, G., & Mai, N. (1991). Problem-solving deficits in brain injured patients: A therapeutic approach. *Neuropsychological Rehabilitation, 1,* 45–64.

Weyandt, L., Iwaszuk, W., Fulton, K., Ollerton, M., Beatty, N., Fouts, H., Schepman, S., & Greenlaw, C. (2003). The internal restlessness scale: Performance of college students with and without DHD. *Journal of Learning Disabilities, 36,* 382–389.

Winocur, G., Palmer, H., Stuss, D. T., Alexander, M. P., Craik, F. I., Levine, B., & Robertson, I. H. (2000). Cognitive rehabilitation in clinical neuropsychology. *Brain and Cognition, 42*(1), 120–123. doi:10.1006/brcg.1999.1179

Woods, S., Lovejoy, D., Stutts, M., Ball, J. D., & Fals-Steward, W. (2002). Comparative efficiency of a discrepancy analysis for the classification of attention-deficit/hyperactivity disorder in adults. *Archives of Clinical Neuropsychology, 17,* 351–369.

CHAPTER 5

STRATEGIES FOR ATHLETE SUCCESS AT HISTORICALLY BLACK COLLEGES AND UNIVERSITIES (HBCUs)

Joseph N. Cooper

ABSTRACT

The purpose of this chapter is to highlight key strategies implemented at historically black colleges and universities (HBCUs) that have contributed to positive developmental outcomes for Black student athletes. Dating back to the mid-19th century, HBCUs have served for Black students as places of opportunity where athletes can develop their talents academically and athletically. The founding principles of these institutions consist of culturally empowering mission statements, purposefully designed programs, and positive institutional relationships. Grounded in previous research, the following five strategies were identified as effective approaches to enhancing Black student athletes' academic achievement at institutions that are members of the National Collegiate Athletic Association (NCAA) Division I and II: (a) early intervention programs, (b) purposefully designed study halls, (c) institution-wide academic support services, (d) public recognition of student athletes' academic accomplishments, and (e) nurturing familial campus climates.

Making the Connection, pages 63–77

INTRODUCTION

Prior to the late-19th century, educational opportunities for Blacks in the United States were significantly limited and oftentimes nonexistent due to the pervasiveness of legalized racism (Gutek, 1986). During that period, Whites controlled nearly every facet of U.S. society and denied Blacks access to various resources including educational institutions. In light of these barriers, Blacks coalesced with different philanthropic and religious organizations (e.g., African Methodist Episcopal [AME] church, Quakers, Presbyterians, American Missionary Association (AMA), Christian Methodist Episcopal (CME) church, Bureau of Refugees, Freedmen's societies, and Abandoned Lands) to form their own schools, which later became known as historically Black colleges and universities (HBCUs) (Fleming, 1984). The first Black colleges were established in progressive Northern states such as Ohio (Wilberforce University in 1856) and Pennsylvania (Cheyney University, formerly the Institute for Colored Youth, in 1837 and Lincoln University, formerly Ashmun Institute, in 1854) (Branson, 1978). After the passage of the second Morrill Land Grant Act, several HBCUs were established through the Southern and mid-Atlantic regions (Fleming, 1984). In fact, a majority of HBCUs were founded in former slaves states (Ladson-Billings, 2012). Between 1854 and 2013, the number of HBCUs in the United States increased from one to 105 (United Negro College Fund, 2013).

Since their inception, HBCUs have implemented effective strategies that facilitate positive developmental outcomes for Black students. The unique mission of HBCUs involves providing quality educational opportunities and experiences for students regardless of their precollege backgrounds (socioeconomic status, academic preparation, race, ethnicity, etc.) (Allen & Jewel, 2002; Brown & Davis, 2001). HBCUs accomplish this mission by creating and enacting culturally-responsive educational practices (e.g., mission statements, formal policies, and informal practices) (Gallien & Peterson, 2005). Moreover, the critical mass of Black faculty, administrators, and staff at these institutions fosters a welcoming campus climate whereby Black students have the opportunity to interact with individuals whom they can identify with racially, ethnically, and socio culturally. In contrast to many predominantly White institutions (PWIs), HBCUs serve as safe havens where Black students experience cultural empowerment and institutional support for their personal development (Allen, 1992; Fleming, 1984).

BLACK STUDENT ATHLETES' EXPERIENCES
AT HBCUs VERSUS PWIs

Previous research on Black student athletes found that HBCUs were better educational environments for these athletes' academic and psycho-social development compared to PWIs (American Institutes for Research, 1988, 1989; Person & LeNoir, 1997; Steinfeldt, Reed, & Steinfeldt, 2010). In 1987, the National Collegiate Athletic Association (NCAA) solicited the American Institutes for Research (AIR) to conduct a series of studies on the effects of participation in intercollegiate athletics at Division I institutions including HBCUs and PWIs (American Institutes for Research, 1988, 1989). The study involved 4,083 participants, including student athletes and student nonathletes, who participated in extracurricular activities from three HBCUs and 39 PWIs. Findings from these studies revealed Black student athletes who attended HBCUs earned higher cumulative grade point averages (GPAs) and reported higher levels of positive psycho-social adjustment compared to those who attended PWIs. More specifically, Black football and men's basketball student athletes who attended HBCUs were less likely to experience social isolation, racial discrimination, and feelings of lack of control over their lives. As one of the first major studies on Black student athletes' experiences, these findings suggested that the educational and sociocultural environments at HBCUs were more effective at meeting the needs of Black student athletes.

In another comparative study, Person and LeNoir (1997) examined the experiences of 31 African-American male student athletes from 11 institutions including nine PWIs and two HBCUs. The authors found faculty–student interactions were more frequent at HBCUs, which led to increased levels of student involvement in research activities and internship programs. In addition, the authors also suggested that student satisfaction was linked to the quality of faculty–student interactions. More recently, Steinfeldt, Reed, and Steinfeldt (2010) examined the racial and athletic identity among African-American football student athletes at three HBCUs and two PWIs. A key finding from this study revealed African-American football student athletes at HBCUs possessed lower levels of athletic identity compared to their peers at PWIs. The authors suggested that the African-American football student athletes at PWIs might have internalize their athletic identity at a higher level when compared to their peers at HBCUs because their athletic identity was valued more at these institutions. Factors such as the over representation of African-American males on athletic teams and the concurrent under representation of African-American males in the general student body served to reinforce the idea that PWIs primarily valued them as athletes (Harper, Williams, & Blackman, 2013). Collectively, the aforementioned studies highlight patterns associated with Black male student athletes' experiences in different educational contexts and indicate HBCUs are more effective than PWIs at meeting their academic and psychosocial needs.

Moreover, data from a NCAA (2009) report revealed student athletes at Division II HBCUs graduated at higher rates than the general student body at these institutions (Hodge, Collins, & Bennett, 2013). At Division II HBCUs, the academic success rates (ASRs) for student athletes was 45.5% compared to 31.8% for the general student body. Given the fact that a majority of the HBCUs in the NCAA are Division II institutions, these statistics are encouraging and suggest athletic participation at HBCUs facilitates positive academic outcomes among Black student athletes.

STRATEGIES FOR ATHLETE SUCCESS AT HBCUs

An emerging body of research has focused on understanding the best practices implemented at HBCUs as it relates to Black student athletes' academic achievement at the NCAA Division I and II level (Charlton, 2011; Cooper, 2013; Cooper & Hawkins, 2012). A review of these data-driven studies reveals five common strategies implemented by HBCUs and their academic support staff that have facilitated positive academic outcomes for their student athletes: (a) early intervention programs, (b) purposefully designed study halls, (c) institution wide academic support services, (d) public recognition of student athletes' academic achievement, and (e) nurturing familial campus climates. Data from these studies will be included in subsequent sections to highlight the effectiveness of these academic support services at HBCUs.

Early Intervention Programs

One effective strategy at HBCUs that has contributed to positive transitional and academic outcomes for Black student athletes has been the implementation of early intervention programs. These early intervention programs acknowledge that the transition from high school to college is challenging for all students, but particularly for student athletes who face the additional obstacles of balancing the responsibilities of full-time student with those of intercollegiate athlete. In a study examining the role of policy, rituals, and language at an academically focused HBCU athletic program, Charlton (2011) found that an early intervention program successfully assisted first-year and transfer student athletes with their transition to South Atlantic University (SAU)[1] (a Division I HBCU). The SAU athletic department's early intervention program consisted of weekly freshman meetings for all first-year and transfer student athletes. The program had five key objectives for participating student athletes: (a) address their transition concerns, (b) develop strong time-management skills, (c) assist with the selection of an academic major related to their interests, (d) introduce them to NCAA compliance rules, and (e) integrate them into the SAU culture. Student athletes in the program were required to meet with the assistant coordinator of academic services or the academic services graduate assistant (GA) every week during their first semester at SAU. At these meetings, student athletes submitted academic folders, which included information about their current courses and accompanying assignments.

The SAU athletic staff cited several reasons for why they felt this program was effective. First, these new student athletes were introduced to key individuals in the academic services program. These one-on-one interactions facilitated the development of meaningful personal relationships between academic services staff and the student athletes. Secondly, these weekly meetings provided academic services staff with the opportunity to identify the areas of need for these student athletes to ensure that they received proper attention to those areas at the beginning of their college careers rather than later. Another important feature of these programs included the involvement of the coaches. Specifically, the head coach was notified of any intervention effort, so the planning process included input from all three parties (student athlete, coach, and academic services staff). Thirdly, the SAU staff felt these meetings were important because they socialized the student athletes at the beginning of the college experience at SAU to the idea that academics were a top priority at the institution. At these meetings, the SAU academic services staff engrained athletes with the motto, "Become a student athlete graduate at SAU," so that they understood and internalized their ultimate purpose at SAU: to acquire an education and graduate (Charlton, 2011, p. 130).

In concert with the SAU athletic staff, the student athletes also indicated that this program was beneficial to them. A major reason cited by the student athletes was the fact that the program keep them accountable and on track academically. The fact that these meetings were scheduled weekly and were a requirement for their athletic eligibility made it easy for the student athletes to incorporate them into their schedules. Furthermore, the SAU academic services staff established another level of accountability by sending weekly email memos to all head coaches and athletic administrators regarding student athletes' attendance records at these meetings. In addition, the student athletes also described how their positive relationships with the academic services staff made them feel supported academically and personally at SAU.

Along the same lines, Cooper and Hawkins (2012) found that Black male student athletes at a Division II HBCU benefited from their participation in an early invention program called TRIO. The TRIO program is a federally funded university-wide academic support program designed to assist students from disadvantaged backgrounds. The TRIO program at Mission University (MU)[2] recruited students to participate in a summer bridge program. Similar to the weekly freshman meetings at SAU, services provided by the TRIO program at MU included transition to college workshops, peer mentoring meetings, and academic training sessions (e.g., college preparatory courses, study habit training). The Black male student athletes who participated described how the programs were helpful because they were able to acclimate to the academic culture at MU and receive the academic attention they needed prior beginning their first full academic year. For example, Kenneth, a freshman football player at MU, described his experience in the TRIO program:

> I'm in TRIO services...student support services...and they came to me when I first got here....I came here in the summer time as a freshman...you know I wasn't doing too good....I had like a 2 point [GPA]...2.5 or something like that...but when I got with them, man, it just helped me...they helped me get my GPA up to a 3.0. (Cooper, 2012, p. 178)

Kenneth's experiences with the TRIO program reflect the importance of early intervention programs for the success of Black student athletes in college. Key features of both the weekly freshman meetings at SAU and the TRIO program at MU were the identification and recruitment of Black student athletes who needed transitional assistance and the delivery of targeted services to meet their unique needs. In addition, the emphasis on academic development and institutional support within these programs signaled to the student athletes that their academic success was a priority at these institutions.

Purposefully Designed Study Halls

Purposefully designed study halls were another strategy HBCUs implemented to foster Black student athletes' academic achievement and personal development. The term *purposefully designed* referred to the strategic implementation of program features including the location of the facility, structure of the schedules, design of the rooms, and the background of the individuals who served as support staff. In Charlton's (2011) study, the administrators, coaches, and student athletes cited the mandatory athletic study hall as one of the most effective academic policies at SAU. Key features of the SAU study hall were its location, structure, consistent enforcement of rules, student athletes' access to academic support staff and resources, and the incentive that exceptional academic performance could exempt them from study hall.

Both the location and structure of the SAU study hall were designed to create a friendly yet structured environment for student athletes (Charlton, 2011, p. 127). The study hall was located in the academic services center at SAU and was divided into two sections. One section was located next to the office of the head coordinator for academic support services, which allowed her to have direct oversight of the daily activities in study hall. In addition to this oversight, the head coordinator of academic support services, whom all the student athletes met during their weekly freshman meetings, had an friendly open-door policy for student athletes, which allowed them meet with her any time to seek advice or simply to have a conversation. This purposeful design of the study hall fostered positive relationships between the student athletes and the academic support services staff. The second section of the study hall was designed to be a space where student athletes could complete their academic tasks individually, in small groups, or with the assistance of the academic support staff. At the entrance to the room, each athlete had to pass an academic support staff member and sign in upon arrival. The assistant coordinator for academic support services was strategically positioned on the opposite side of the room from the sign-in staff person to ensure effective monitoring of student athletes' activities.

Inside these rooms, student athletes had access to individual desks, group study tables, and computer hubs to help them complete their academic tasks. All freshman and transfer student athletes had to attend the study hall at least four, 1-hr sessions, which translated into roughly 52 hr per semester. Student athletes with 2.4 GPAs or lower were also required to attend four, 1-hr sessions of study hall each week and participate in a developmental course focused on building positive academic habits. To minimize distractions during study hall, all social networking sites were blocked, cell phone usage was prohibited, and loud talking was not allowed. Every Friday, the head coordinator for academic support services sent out an email to a group of athletic administrators and coaches informing them about student athletes' attendance and behavior at study hall. If necessary, coaches would reinforce disciplinary actions on any student athletes who were found to be noncompliant with study-hall policies. Collectively, the purposefully designed features of the SAU study hall provided student athletes with a structured support system to assist them with their academic development.

In another study, Cooper (2013) examined the key influences associated with the academic achievement and college experiences of Black male student athletes at a Division II HBCU and found that the location and design of the study hall were beneficial to meeting the student athletes' academic needs. Similarly the location of the SAU academic services center, the athletic study hall at Northern Central University (NCU)[3] was strategically located along the same hallway as the athletic department and health, physical education, and recreation academic department offices, which facilitated oversight by faculty and administrators. There were four rooms designated for athletic study hall at NCU: Two of the rooms were equipped with computers and the other two rooms were large classroom spaces with 35 desks each, two whiteboards, and four large tables.

During study hall, there were academic counselors including academic support staff, graduate teaching assistants, and undergraduate peer tutors, who were in charge of monitoring study hall activities. All student athletes were required to sign in with the head academic counselor upon arrival and to sign out upon departure. A unique feature of the NCU study hall was the fact that all student athletes were required to complete 10 hr per week of study hall both in season and out of season. The Black male student athletes in the study indicated that they benefitted from having to attend study hall year round because it signaled to them that academics was a priority regardless of their athletic commitments. The study hall operated seven days a week, which was also purposefully designed to accommodate student athletes' hectic schedules. Participants also felt the effective monitoring of study hall created a sense of accountability not only to themselves, but also to their academic support staff, coaches, and teammates.

Another key feature of study halls that Black male student athletes at HBCUs have highlighted as beneficial was the presence of peer tutors (Cooper, 2013; Cooper & Hawkins, 2012). Participants in Cooper and Hawkins' (2012) study described how their peer tutors connected with them and understood their unique schedules as student athletes. The MU academic support services worked diligently to ensure student athletes had access to peer tutors who possessed subject-area expertise so as to optimize support efforts. Similarly, Cooper (2013) found Black male student athletes at NCU felt it was helpful to have a peer communicate academic concepts to them in a way that was easier to understand than their professors' delivery in class. Several participants had difficulty grasping the material reviewed in class by the professor given the time constraints, but meeting with peer tutors outside of class gave them time to ask questions. As a result, the purposeful efforts regarding the location, structure, design, and selection of academic support staff contributed to positive academic outcomes for Black student athletes at HBCUs.

Institution-Wide Academic Support Programs

Another effective strategy for Black student athletes' academic success practiced at HBCUs was the presence of well-coordinated interdepartmental academic support programs. At SAU (Charlton, 2011) and MU (Cooper & Hawkins, 2012), the athletic departments had their own academic support staff who worked in concert with the faculty, academic advising office, university-wide academic support center, and office of student affairs at their respective institutions to provide comprehensive support to student athletes. For example, at SAU, the athletic department's head coordinator for academic support services oversaw all student athletes' initial academic advising (Charlton, 2011). Since all student athletes were required to participate in the weekly freshman meetings, the head coordinator was well aware of the student athletes' academic needs as well as their progress towards degree completion. Therefore, this pre-established relationship allowed for optimal assistance with course enrollment, academic major selection, and the dropping of courses. After student athletes met with the head coordinator for academic support services they would meet with their university assigned academic advisor to register for their courses. Within this effort, both the head coordinator for academic support services and the university academic advising staff collaborated to ensure student athletes remained on track for graduation and enrolled in academic majors congruent with their interests.

Similarly, Cooper, and Hawkins (2012) also found Black male student athletes at MU benefitted from campus-wide academic support programs. In addition to the TRIO program, participants highlighted the MU writing center as an effective academic support service. One reason for its effectiveness was the one-on-one attention student athletes received from the MU writing center staff. Participants described how the staff would take time to explain and address the areas needing improvement. Another benefit of this program was the MU writing center's central location in the main part of campus. This intentional location facilitated Black male student athletes' integration into the campus community, which reminded them that their role as a student took precedent over their athletic participation.

Moreover, Cooper (2013) found that Black male student athletes at NCU greatly benefitted from participating in a university-wide academic support program called the academic study tables. The office of student affairs and the academic retention center at NCU operated this program, but these offices also worked in conjunction with the athletic department to ensure optimal athlete participation in the program. The program was designed to provide students with a structured environment to complete their academic tasks and receive academic assistance. Participants highlighted three main features of the academic study tables program that contributed to their academic achievement. The first feature was the opportunity to receive assistance from their professors and peer tutors. The program was designed based on previous research, which found students tended to perform better academically when they spent at least 2 hr a day studying, were involved in peer study groups, and spent time outside of class with a professor or tutor. The fact that professors attended these sessions reflected the program's importance at NCU. Furthermore, the one-on-one interactions with peer tutors were also helpful to Black male student athletes. Participants indicated that having the time to ask additional questions and work through problems was quite beneficial to them.

Another key feature of the academic study tables program was the fact that it was centrally located on campus. Instead of being situated near or in an athletic facility, the program was positioned near the main library and student union, which was convenient for students. In addition, the location sent the message to student athletes that they were students first and athletes second. The third unique feature of the program was its year-round, seven-day-a-week schedule, which allowed student athletes to attend throughout the academic year. Collectively, the presence of well-coordinated, university-wide support programs provided comprehensive academic support to Black student athletes at HBCUs and reinforced that their academic success was valued and important.

Public Recognition of Student Athletes' Academic Accomplishments

Beyond the accolades student athletes received from media outlets for their athletic accomplishments, several HBCUs also recognized student athletes for their academic achievements at an annual award banquets. For example, at SAU the athletic department sponsored a yearend athletic banquet to honor student athletes who had excelled academically as well as those who had performed well athletically (Charlton, 2011). At this event, the most decorated awards were given to the male and female athlete who earned the highest GPAs over the course of the academic year. The athletic director purposefully designed this award to be the most elegant because she wanted to send the message that academic excellence was more important than athletic performance. This award was also strategically presented at the end of the banquet to emphasize the significance of this accomplishment. Another form of public recognition for academic success performed at SAU occurred annually at a home basketball game during the spring semester, where student athletes who earned a 3.0 GPA or higher during the previous semester were honored. The SAU president conducted the ceremony and presented certificates to all recipients, who were accompanied by their respective head coaches. All student athletes were required to attend this ceremony, and business attire was the dress code.

At NCU, the athletic department also sponsored an annual sports banquet every April to honor the academic and athletic achievements of its student athletes (Cooper, 2013). All student athletes were required to attend this banquet. Each head coach selected award recipients based on university, athletic department, and team expectations. All scholar athletes who earn a 3.0 GPA or higher were honored at this event. NCU was also an institutional member of the National Student Athlete Honors Society and recognized all juniors and seniors who earn a 3.4 GPA or higher. Similar to SAU, the academic awards for the student athletes who earned the highest GPAs were the most decorated. The recognition of academic achievement at these award banquets and ceremonies served as a public acknowledgement that these institutions valued academic success and, more importantly, provided an incentive for all student athletes to put forth their best efforts academically.

Nurturing Familial Campus Environments

The most important strategy for student athletes' success at HBCUs has been the presence of nurturing familial campus environments. These environments were created through culturally responsive policies and by caring faculty, administrators, and staff. More specifically, institutional actors at HBCUs engaged in what Hirt, Amelink, McFeeters, and Strayhorn (2008) described as *other mothering*, whereby these individuals treated their students as their own children and provided them with holistic guidance and support beyond traditional academic advisement (p. 217). At SAU, various institutional staff members engaged in both verbal and non-verbal behaviors that created a familial environment for the student athletes (Charlton, 2011). The head coordinator for academic support services engaged in other mothering by talking with student athletes about non-academic issues and demonstrating a genuine interest in their well-being beyond their academic needs. She would also affectionately refer to all of her student athletes as "sweetie" and greet them with hugs whenever they entered into the academic services center. Another way the familial campus climate was established at SAU was through the president's regular attendance at athletic home games and his interactions with the student athletes, which revealed his commitment to building personal relationships with the student athletes. These collective actions by the various administrators and staff reflected the nurturing familial environment at SAU and contributed to positive college experiences for the student athletes. One of the student athletes captured the impact of this familial culture when he said: "Knowing people care . . . you don't want to let them down" (Charlton, 2011, p. 138).

Using a grounded theory approach to analysis, Cooper and Hawkins (2012) used findings from their study to propose a nurturing community hypothesis (NCH), which refers to "an educational environment that contributes positive student-athlete outcomes through the promotion of holistic identity development in policy and practice" (Cooper & Hawkins, 2012, p. 183). At HBCUs, the mission statements and policies explicitly placed an emphasis on the holistic development of Black students through strong institutional relationships. At MU, the nurturing and supportive faculty, administrators, and staff cultivated a familial culture that reinforced positive identities among Black male student athletes. The critical mass of Black faculty, administrators, and staff signaled to Black male students athletes that they not only belonged at MU, but they were capable of success in areas other than athletics. The small classes at MU also fostered a climate for the development of meaningful and positive relationships. Participants talked about how their professors knew them by name and expressed a sincere interest in their well-being aside from academics. Similarly, coaches established a bond with their student athletes that extended beyond athletics. These intentional acts of care reflected MU's mission of developing students' holistically.

Cooper (2013) also identified effective nurturing strategies implemented at NCU that contributed to positive outcomes for Black male student athletes. Specifically cited as best practices were the establishment of positive faculty–student relationships and culturally empowering campus events (e.g., annual homecomings). Regarding faculty–student interactions, the Black male student athletes at NCU highlighted how their professors displayed an ethic of care toward them by meeting with them outside of class, understanding their unique schedules as student athletes, and talking with them about non-academic issues. In addition, participants expressed how culturally empowering events, such as the annual homecomings, enhanced their collective identity with NCU and enhanced their institutional commitment. Everyone from the NCU president, alumni, faculty, administrators, staff, students, and local community members participated in these events to celebrate institutional pride, cultural celebration, and athletic tradition (Lillig, 2009).

At NCU, there were two annual homecomings, one held during football season and the other during basketball season. Participants highlighted how the camaraderie during these events had been a unique experience that enhanced their collective identity with the school. At these events, Black cultural empowerment, expression, and unity were on display (Archer & Watson, 2005). Various activities at these events included the historic battle of the bands, step shows, fashion shows, parades, tailgating, professional workshops, and community service outreach (Moore, 2012). Institutions seeking to enhance Black male student athletes' college experiences and levels of engagement should consider sponsoring culturally empowering events that reflect an appreciation and celebration of Black culture. These symbolic events create a level of cultural responsiveness, and signal to Black students' that their heritage is important and valued.

CONCLUSION

Historically HBCUs have been successful at cultivating positive educational environments for Black students, by being sensitive to their unique needs, upholding high expectations for personal behavior, and providing adequate support to help them over societal and individual challenges (Allen & Jewel, 2002; Kim, 2002; Kim & Conrad, 2006; Nettles & Perna, 1997; Palmer & Gasman, 2008). Despite the widespread criticism of the HBCUs as unfit educational institutions for the 21st century, this chapter highlights the important role these institutions fulfill in terms of providing quality educational opportunities and experiences for Black male student athletes. Collectively, the presence of culturally-empowering missions, purposefully-designed programs, and an institutional commitment to student athletes' holistic development are key strategies for their success in college and beyond.

QUESTIONS FOR DISCUSSION

1. How is the mission of HBCUs unique from other institutions of higher education?
2. Should the academic success metrics (e.g., graduation rates, academic progress rates) be the same for all institutions regardless of their mission statements, admission standards, and financial resources? Why or why not?
3. Should HBCUs exist in the 21st century as they are currently structured? If so, why? If not, why not?
4. Why do Black student athletes graduate at higher rates compared to student non athletes at HBCUs?
5. What role do university or college presidents, faculty, administrators, and staff play in the cultivation of positive educational environments for Black student athletes?
6. What factors contribute to the differences between Black student athletes' experiences at HBCUs compared to PWIs?

NOTES

1. A pseudonym was used to preserve the anonymity of the institution and participants. This pseudonym was used in the original article.
2. A pseudonym was used to preserve the anonymity of the institution and participants. This pseudonym was used in the original article.
3. A pseudonym was assigned to the institution to preserve anonymity.

REFERENCES

Allen, W. R. (1992). The color of success: African-American college student outcomes at predominantly White and historically Black public colleges and universities. *Harvard Educational Review, 62*(1), 26–44.

Allen, W. R., & Jewel, J. O. (2002). A backward glance forward: Past, present, and future perspectives on historically Black colleges and universities. *Review of Higher Education, 25*(3), 241–261.

American Institutes for Research. (1988). Summary results from the 1987–1988 national study of intercollegiate athletics. *Studies in Intercollegiate Athletics.* Palo Alto, CA: Center for the Study of Athletics.

American Institutes for Research. (1989). The experiences of Black intercollegiate athletes at NCAA Division I institutions. *Studies in Intercollegiate Athletics.* Palo Alto, CA: Center for the Study of Athletics.

Archer, S., & Watson, J. C. (2005). Samuel Archer and J. B. Watson on football at Southern Black colleges. In D. K. Wiggins & P. B. Wiggins (Eds.), *The unleveled playing field: A documentary history of the African-American experience in sport* (pp. 43–45). Urbana, IL: University of Illinois Press.

Branson, H. R. (1978). Black colleges of the North. In C. V. Willie & R. R. Edmonds (Eds.), *Black colleges in America.* New York, NY: Teachers College Press.

Brown, M. C., & Davis, J. E. (2001). The historically Black college as social contract, social capital, and social equalizer. *Peabody Journal of Education, 76*(1), 31–49.

Charlton, R. (2011). The role of policy, rituals, and language in shaping an academically focused culture in HBCU athletics. *Journal of Issues in Intercollegiate Athletics, 4,* 120–148.

Cooper, J. N. (2013). *A mixed methods exploratory study of Black male student athletes' experiences at a historically Black university.* [Doctoral dissertation. Department of Kinesiology, University of Georgia, Athens, GA.]

Cooper, J. N., & Hawkins, B. (2012). A place of opportunity: Black male student athletes' experiences at a historically Black university. *Journal of Intercollegiate Sport, 5,* 170–188.

Fleming, J. (1984). *Blacks in college.* San Francisco, CA: Jossey-Bass.

Gallien, L. B., Jr., & Peterson, M. S. (2005). *Instructing and mentoring the African-American college student: Strategies for success in higher education.* Boston, MA: Pearson Education.

Gutek, G. L. (1986). *Education in the United States: A historical perspective.* Englewood Cliffs, NJ: Prentice-Hall

Harper, S. R., Williams, C. D., & Blackman, H. W. (2013). *Black male student athletes and racial inequities in NCAA Division I college sports.* Philadelphia, PA: University of Pennsylvania, Center for the Study of Race and Equity in Education.

Hirt, J. B., Amelink, C. A., McFeeters, B. B., & Strayhorn, T. L. (2008). A system of other mothering: Student affairs administrators' perceptions of relationships with students at historically Black colleges. *NASPA* (National Association of Student Personnel Administrators), *45*(2), 210–236.

Hodge, S. R., Collins, F. G., & Bennett, I., R. A. (2013). The journey of the Black athlete on the HBCU playing field. In D. Brooks & R. Althouse (Eds.),

Racism in college athletics (pp. 105–133). Morgantown, WV: Fitness Information Technology.

Kim, M. M. (2002). Historically Black vs. White institutions: Academic development among Black students. *Review of Higher Education, 25*, 385–407.

Kim, M. M., & Conrad, C. F. (2006). The impact of historically Black colleges and universities on the academic success of African-American students. *Research in Higher Education, 47*, 399–427.

Ladson-Billings, G. (2012). Through a glass darkly: The persistence of race in education research and scholarship. *Educational Researcher, 41*(4), 115–120.

Lillig, J. (2009). "Magic" or misery: HBCUs, guarantee contracts, and public policy. *Journal of Sports Law & Contemporary Problems, 6*(41), 41–71.

Moore, E. (2012). "Black college football classic games: A taste of the HBCU athletic experience." Retrieved from http://www.collegeview.com/articles/article/black-college-football-classic-games

NCAA. (2009). Division I graduation success rate/Division II academic success rate (NCAA, Trans.). Retrieved from http://www.ncaa.org/about/resources/research/graduation-success-rate

Nettles, M. T., & Perna, L. W. (1997). *The African-American education data book, Vol. 1: Higher and adult education.* Fairfax, VA: Frederick D. Patterson Research Institute of The College Fund/UNCF.

Palmer, R., & Gasman, M. (2008). It takes a village to raise a child: The role of social capital in promoting academic success for African-American men at a Black college. *Journal of College Student Development, 49*(1), 52–70.

Person, D. R., & LeNoir, K. M. (1997). Retention issues and models for African-American male athletes. *New Directions for Student Services, 80*, 79–91.

Steinfeldt, J. A., Reed, C., & Steinfeldt, M. C. (2010). Racial and athletic identity of African-American football players at historically Black colleges and universities and predominantly White institutions. *Journal of Black Psychology, 36*(1), 3–24.

United Negro College Fund. (2013). "About HBCUs." Retrieved from http://www.uncf.org/sections/MemberColleges/SS_AboutHBCUs/about.hbcu.asp

CHAPTER 6

AN OVERVIEW OF DATA-INFORMED STRATEGIES THAT SELF-AFFIRM COLLEGE ATHLETE IDENTITIES

Scholar Baller as the Ideal and Goal Destination of Success

C. Keith Harrison and Janet Rasmussen

ABSTRACT

Colleges and universities incorporate academic motivational programs to help combat low-academic performance. One unique program, Scholar Baller, utilizes popular culture within its curriculum to bridge the gap between academics and athletics, and to affirm identities in a culturally responsive way. The mission of Scholar Baller is to inspire young adults to excel in education as well as life by using their cultural interests in sports and entertainment. This chapter does the following with the Scholar Baller mission statement as a con-

Making the Connection, pages 79–90
Copyright © 2015 by Information Age Publishing
All rights of reproduction in any form reserved.

duit: (a) examines the current academic literature on self-affirmation theories, (b) addresses a three-part question centered on approaches to engage and re-engage college athletes, (c) outlines best practices of self-affirmation, and (d) highlights two case studies of game changers in terms of Scholar Baller partnerships with the Jordan clothing brand and the National Football League Player Engagement department.

INTRODUCTION

Less than 3% of college athletes go on to play sports professionally, thus it is important that they are prepared for careers outside of athletics (Stewart, 2008). There are numerous Division I football players specifically that have low grade-point averages and graduation rates. Academic motivational programs have been incorporated by universities to help combat low academic performance. One unique program, Scholar Baller, uses popular culture to make a connection between academics and athletics, and to affirm culturally responsive identities (Morrell & Duncan-Andrade, 2006). The mission of Scholar Baller is to inspire excellence in education, as well as life, by using young adults' cultural interests in sports and entertainment. Using the Scholar Baller mission statement as a conduit, this chapter will: (a) examine the current academic literature on self-affirmation theories, (b) address a three-part question centered on approaches to engage and re-engage college athletes, (c) outline best practices of self-affirmation, and (d) highlight two case studies of game changers in terms of Scholar-Baller partnerships with the Jordan clothing brand and the National Football League Player Engagement department.

SUCCESS AND SELF-AFFIRMATION:
ACADEMICS, ATHLETICS, AND IDENTITY

In our society, individuals are faced with threats to their integrity every day (Cohen, Garcia, Apfel, & Master, 2006). These threats can involve many different standards of integrity: intelligence, control over important outcomes, being a good member of a group, or anything important to an individual (Leary & Baumeister, 2000). By focusing on different important identities and values, it has been shown that individuals can become less defensive toward threatening information. This different psychological approach involves self-affirmation theory. Self-affirmation theory was developed by Claude Steele in 1988 to explain the premise that individuals strive to maintain their self-integrity. When negative feedback occurs, according to Steele (1988), individuals are motivated to protect their self-worth. Making individuals aware of other important values they hold unrelated to the threat, negates the connection to their self-worth (Cohen, 2006; Crocker, Niiya & Mischkowski, 2008).

Self-affirming in one area reduces the need to defend in another area (Armitage, Harris, Napper, & Hepton, 2008). When self-affirmed, an individual can become more confident, open minded and receptive (Cohen, 2006). A self-affirming exercise includes completing a scale or writing exercise on an important personal value (Cohen, 2006). A person needs to affirm values that are meaningful to them (Tesser, 2000). Therefore, if athletes complete a writing exercise about what their athletic scholarship means to them, they may protect their self-integrity and feel more positive towards other critical areas in their lives such as academic performance. Studies have suggested that by participating in self-affirming activities, athletes are more engaged in their learning (Kumashiro & Sedikides, 2005; Steele, 1988), and they respond more positively to negative academic feedback.

Another interesting study regarding self-affirmation suggests that engaging in value-affirming exercises can possibly engender feelings of caring for other people or things (Crocker & Mischkowski, 2008). Whether self-image is boosted by these exercises, or a person is reminded of other people or things beyond themselves, self-affirmation exercises seem to have a positive effect. Koole, Smeets, Van Knippenberg and Dijksterhuis (1999) state that self-affirmation promotes trivialization of a blocked goal. By increasing the salience of a personal value, it becomes easier for the person to compare the importance of the blocked goal and the personal value. After comparison, the blocked goal is seen to have less significance and therefore the person finds it easier to address the goal blockage (Koole et al., 1999).

College athletes are one group that faces goal blockage, as well as negative stereotypes in the classroom (Harrison, 2007). According to Crocker et al., (2008), the academic domain may be especially threatening to athletes. This stressful environment can cause athletes to create goal blockage (Koole et al., 1999). However, through self-affirmation exercises, athletes can feel better about themselves, and be more willing to accept criticism. College athletes may become more open minded and not relate the academic criticism to negative stereotyping, such as racism or "dumb jock" (Cohen, 2006; Crocker et al.). Self-affirmation acts as a framework in which an athlete can overcome negative stereotypes and increase academic performance (Cohen). By protecting self-integrity, an athlete will be able to accept threatening experiences and information and can sustain optimism and effort, which will allow for a positive change to occur (Cohen).

In the final analysis, self-affirmation theory is an effective framework for scholars and practitioners who seek to understand athlete populations. Self-affirmation is the foundation of the Scholar-Baller curriculum used to facilitate culturally responsive pedagogy with various student populations at the high school, community college, and four-year university levels. In terms of athletic identity, this framework has been utilized in a series of studies that are summarized in the next section.

Synthesis of Studies Related to Self-Affirmation With Athletic Populations

In a study of football players at four universities (i.e., two Scholar-Baller and two non Scholar-Baller universities), Rasmussen (2009) found that Scholar-Baller athletes had significantly higher athletic identity than non Scholar-Baller football players, and these Scholar-Baller schools achieved high overall team GPA and graduation rates. Moreover, there were no significant differences when comparing African American, White American and other race or ethnicity across academic, athletic, intrinsic motivation, and athletic identity areas; however when comparing African Americans and White Americans there were significant differences.

Relatedly, Harrison and Stone (2009) conducted an experiment to examine factors that moderate the experience of an academic identity threat among college athletes, who represent a stigmatized group on most college campuses. It was hypothesized that because they are more engaged in academics, female college athletes would be especially threatened by the prospect of confirming the dumb-jock stereotype. As predicted, female college athletes performed more poorly when their athletic and academic identities were explicitly linked, but only on moderately difficult test items. The results also revealed that male college athletes performed significantly better on more difficult test items when only their athletic identity was primed prior to the test. This is an important finding, as there is little research on the impact of positive stereotypes on performance. The discussion focuses on the different motivational processes (i.e., self-affirmation) that impact the academic performance of male and female college athletes when aspects of their campus identity are primed within a classroom context. This poses the question: how does race factor into academic and athletic identities on campus?

Furthermore, Stone, Harrison, and Mottley (2012) found that academically engaged African-American college athletes are most susceptible to stereotype threat in the classroom when the context links their unique status as both scholar and athlete. After completing a measure of academic engagement, African-American and White college athletes completed a test of verbal reasoning. To vary stereotype threat, they first indicated their status on the cover page as a scholar athlete, an athlete, or as a research participant. Compared to the other groups, academically engaged African-American college athletes performed poorly on the difficult test items when primed for their athletic identity, but they performed worse on both the difficult and easy test items when primed for their identity as a scholar-athlete. The unique stereotype threat processes that affect the academic performance of minority college athletes were discussed.

These specific research investigations enable the authors of this chapter to articulate some of the practical approaches that student-affairs leaders who frequently work with this special population of students might implement.

Three-Tier Approach on Campus

1. How might scholars and practitioners spark conversation about ways college and university constituents can reframe their thinking about the importance of innovative research to inform practices?

The term student athlete is stagnate and it is imperative that this term be put in a historical context (Staurowsky & Sack, 2005). The language and linguistic constructions we use with athletic populations must be relevant and communicate the message of *balance* in terms of academic success coupled with athletic responsibilities while on campus. Scholar Baller, Athletes Think, and Academic Swagger are just a few labels that affirm the culture of today's college athlete and that cross the boundaries of gender, race, and social class. Research should examine what terms today's college athlete most identifies with (Harrison & Sutton, 2013).

In order to reframe our thinking, we must take risks and move closer to the culture of today's athletes. This means understanding their worldviews, and engaging them in their post-modern world of technology (e.g., Twitter, Facebook, Instagram). Research should gather qualitative and quantitative data from these social and cultural spaces, as the content on these platforms gives us a broader understanding of the everyday lives of women and men that participate in sports and higher education.

Innovative interactions are important when thinking about mentoring and about leaders being exemplars of professionalism. There is a fine line to walk, but as mentors we must show young adults that we are just a generation, or less, removed from their realities. Research should involve the perspectives of athletes to guide us in part and meet them halfway.

2. How might academic-support stakeholders inspire a greater awareness and action among higher-education practitioners?

Branding the success of athletes is beneficial for players, coaches, parents, faculty, advisors, students, fans, alumni, staff, and other campus stakeholders. We must begin to create a system of highlighting "airplanes that land safely" (Juan et al., 2008) by not telling just the positive stories of athletic success, but rather add more colors (content) to the existing paintbrush that we use in the narratives about college athletes. In other words, they are more than just athletes.

At the 2013 National Association of Academic Advisors for Athletics (N4A) conference, a session called Incentivizing and Marketing Student-Athlete Academic Success provided a platform for roughly 60 professionals and leaders on college campuses to discuss culturally relevant strategies that motivate athletes to excel academically and that recognize athletes for their academic performance. The session allowed for a sharing of best practices in terms of self-affirming messages of educational excellence by athletes, and what approaches academic support leaders used to provide this information to the campus and institutional culture.

Peer mentoring provides a great way to self-affirm constructive academic behaviors by athletes; one way in contemporary society to do this is through social media. In other words, athletes can use Twitter, Facebook, and Instagram to discourse about academics and careers, to fully engage with professors or students, and to engage in intellectual campus activities that are focused on educational achievement.

3. How might our higher-education community of scholars and researchers advance research in this content area?

An important area to consider for future studies includes choice, and the role it plays in athletes' academic and athletic motivation. Investigations of the parents' role in college athletes' choices and motivations are necessary to help further explicate athletes' motivation and identity. Studies involving middle-school and high-school athletes and their parents may help researchers determine other factors involved in athletes' motivation. The field of sports and higher education also needs additional studies on retention programs and how they self-affirm academic excellence and academic improvement. The Scholar-Baller program should be compared to other retention programs used in higher education to increase focus on what strategies work to increase athletes' motivation. Additionally, as motivation can change at any given time, it is important to investigate this in a longitudinal study. Comparison of academic data (grade point averages and graduation rates) to motivation may provide insight into motivation's role in athletes' academic performance. Furthermore, studying a large population of athletes, including those in a variety of men and women's sports, may help contribute to the research literature. However, it is necessary to separate revenue and non-revenue sports as each may have distinct cultures that affect athletes' motivation.

Academic performance success must be seen as part of the identity of the athlete versus an added obligation to their list of priorities. Quantitative data is plentiful in terms of SAT/ACT, GSR, and APR scores. But we need a more systemic analysis of non-cognitive factors and how these influence academic performance and self-affirming behaviors (Sedlacek, 2004). Qualitative data research designs have increased over the last decade with some interesting work on college athletes. However, more research is needed in terms of women and ethnic groups outside the Black/White binary and cultural frame. Narrative perspectives are always important, and this work must evolve into social media spaces where athletes are engaged and likewise might share the visual content of their academic and intellectual identities.

SELF-AFFIRMATION:
BEST PRACTICES FOR COLLEGE ATHLETES

Figure 6.1　First place winners (trophy and certificate). *Note:* A trophy for academic achievement should be comparable to the Heisman Award. *Source:* Photos courtesy of the Paul Robeson Research Center for Academic and Athletic Prowess.

Figure 6.2 Second place winners (coin and certificate). *Note:* Symbols of academic success are important to the identity formation and academic validation of student-athletes from all different backgrounds and various sports. *Source:* Photo courtesy of the Paul Robeson Research Center for Academic and Athletic Prowess.

Figure 6.3 Third place winners (coin and certificate). *Source:* Photo courtesy of the Paul Robeson Research Center for Academic and Athletic Prowess.

After five years of research and brainstorming, the Jordan clothing brand and Scholar Baller (SB) formally partnered in April 2013 on an initiative to impact the cultural landscape of academics, athletics, style, and identity coolness. The partnership had mutually inclusive values in terms of constructs of everyday lifestyles and the impact on identity and fashion. The Jordan brand is

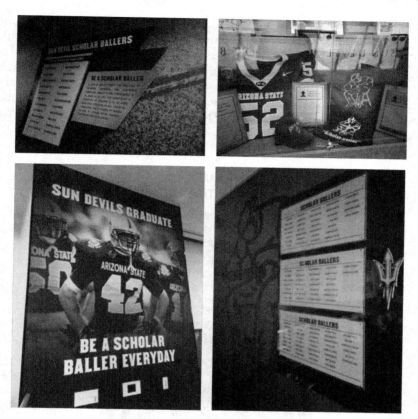

Figure 6.4 A staple in the Scholar-Baller movement is the message of academic success via the patch, helmet sticker, or logo in cultural spaces. *Source:* Photos courtesy of ASU and the Paul Robeson Research Center for Academic and Athletic Prowess

considered one of the coolest clothing lines in the world with consumers from all walks of life, especially athletes that play football and men's and women's basketball. The partnership focused on affirming academic and athletic identities through athletes that achieve at a higher or improved level. Schools that participated in the Scholar-Baller program rewarded high-achieving players with *swag* (gear) that was cobranded with both organizations (see Figure 6.4).

Brief Case Study of Affirmation: National Football League Player Engagement

In February 2013 the National Football League Player Engagement (NFLPE) and Scholar Baller programs formally entered into a partnership to engage the world in a new discourse on how academics, athletics, and career transition are perceived regarding football players and other athletic participants in the United States and the world. Initiatives included highlighting the Scholar Ballers of the month at the NFL, NCAA, NAIA, NJCAA, and most importantly high school and lower levels. By affirming athletes at all levels on a platform (such as the NFLPE's website), youth and young adults across generations now had a way to level the playing field for making it to the pro ranks.

CONCLUSIONS:
WE HAVE TO AFFIRM THAT SCHOOL IS COOL!

Figure 6.5 Chris Bass graduated from LSU in 2012, former AMA Einner. *Source:* Photo courtesy of LSU and Paul Robeson Research Center for Academic and Athletic Prowess.

In the chapter by Harrison and Sutton (2013), *Cracking their world: Utilizing pop culture to impact academic success of today's student-athlete*, Brooks and Althouse (2013) note:

> The authors offer a refreshing look at the intersection of pop culture, athletic participation, and academic success. They introduce concepts focusing on self-affirmation, like the cultural concept of cool and cool pose to help understand and appreciate the African-American male culture and media images. This sets the stage for two very important questions: Is it possible to create

more balance and synergy between the player and his/her academic performance as a student in American higher education? If so, how can academic institutions and individual stakeholders proactively implement programs and strategies to utilize pop culture to improve academic performance? (p. 401)

These two questions have been answered in part in the current chapter, to recap the following, as we: (a) examined the current academic literature on self-affirmation theories, (b) addressed a three-part question centered on approaches to engage and re-engage athletes, (c) observed the best practices of self-affirmation, and (d) analyzed two case studies of game-changers in terms of Scholar-Baller partnerships with the Jordan apparel brand and the National Football League Player Engagement department.

Finally, how do we affirm school being cool on a macro and structural level using all cultural forces available? As a national and hopefully global sports world, we have to move the conversation about academics and athletics to the forefront of the visual presentation of what matters to the given eye. This chapter makes a valiant attempt to demonstrate some of the best practices of Scholar Baller to highlight some of the macro, micro, and structural levels of cultural forces to achieve its educational goals. Time will only tell if this vision is realized.

QUESTIONS FOR DISCUSSION

1. How do self-affirmation theories inform the best practices of academic advisors for athletics?
2. How can social media be maximized and utilized in an innovative way to listen to athletes and collect narrative data in terms of their academic achievements and educational experiences on campus?
3. How does the Academic Momentum Award sponsored by Scholar Baller and the NCAS relate in a practical way to the concept of self-affirmation?
4. What does the future hold for athletes in terms of how our society and higher-education systems affirm their academic performance through athletic prowess?

REFERENCES

Armitage, C. J., Harris, P. R., Napper, L., & Hepton, G. (2008). Efficacy of a brief intervention to increase acceptance of health risk information among adult smokers with low socioeconomic status. *The Psychology of Addictive Behaviors, 22*, 88–95.

Brooks, D. D., & Althouse, R. C. (2013). *Racism in college athletics*. Fitness Information Technology.

Cohen, G., Garcia, J., Apfel, N., & Master, A. (2006). Reducing the racial achievement gap: A social-psychological intervention. *Science, 313*, 1307–1310.

Crocker, J., Niiya, Y., & Mischkowski, D. (2008). Why does writing about important values reduce defensiveness? Self-affirmation and the role of positive other-directed feelings. *Psychological Science, 19*, 740–747.

Harrison, C. K. (2007). Drop it like it's hot: Releasing Scholar-Baller voices and changing the "character of the discourse" in North American post-secondary institutions. *Journal for the Study of Sports and Athletes in Education, 1*(1), 77–88.

Harrison, C. K., & Stone, J. (2009). The role of gender identities and stereotype salience with the academic performance of male and female college athletes. *Journal of Sport and Social Issues, 33*(1), 78–96

Harrison, C. K., & Sutton, W. A. (2013). Cracking their world: Utilizing pop culture to impact academic success of today's student athlete (pp. 255–267). In D. Brooks and R. Althouse (Eds.). *Racism in college athletics (3rd edition)*. Morgantown, WV: Fitness Information Technology.

Juan, C. H., Muggleton, N. G., Tzeng, O. J. L., Hung, D. L., Cowey, A., & Walsh, V. (2008). Segregation of visual selection and saccades in human frontal eye fields. *Cerebral Cortex, 18*, 2410–2415.

Koole, S. L., Smeets, K., Van Knippenberg, A., & Dijksterhuis, A. (1999). The cessation of rumination through self-affirmation. *Journal of Personality and Social Psychology, 77*(1), 111–125.

Kumashiro, M., & Sedikidus, C. (2005). Taking on board liability-focused information: Close positive relationships as a self-bolstering resource. *Psychological Science, 16*, 732–739.

Leary, M., & Baumeister, R. (2000). The nature and function of self-esteem: Sociometer theory. *Advances in experimental social psychology, 32*(1), 1–62.

Morrell, E., & Duncan-Andrade, J. (2006). Popular culture and critical media pedagogy in secondary literacy classrooms. *International Journal of Learning, 12*(9).

Rasmussen, J. (2009). *An investigation of Scholar Baller and non Scholar Baller Division I football student-athletes' academic, athletic, intrinsic motivation, and athletic identity*. [Doctoral dissertation], University of Central Florida, Orlando, FL.

Sedlacek, W. E. (2004). *Beyond the big test: Noncognitive assessment in higher education*. San Francisco, CA: Jossey-Bass.

Staurowsky, E. J., & Sack, A. L. (2005). Reconsidering the use of the term student athlete in academic research. *Journal of Sport Management, 19*(2), 103–116.

Steele, C. M. (1988). The psychology of self-affirmation: Sustaining the integrity of the self. *Advances in experimental social psychology, 21*, 261–302.

Stewart, C. (2008). Clarifying athletic program objectives. *Coach & Athletic Director*. Retrieve from http://www.thefreelibrary.com/

Stone, J., Harrison C. K., & Mottley, J. (2012). Don't call me a student athlete: The effect of identity priming on stereotype threat for academically engaged African American college athletes. *Basic and Applied Social Psychology 34*, 99–106.

Tesser, A. (2000). On the confluence of self-esteem maintenance mechanisms. *Personality and Social Psychology Review, 4*, 290–299.

CHAPTER 7

PREPARATION FOR LIFE AFTER SPORT

Data-Informed Practices for College-Athlete Career Development Programs

Kristina M. Navarro

ABSTRACT

The commercialization of Division I athletics in American society continues to situate college athletic departments as the front porch to large research institutions (Croissant, 2001). Due to the enhanced media scrutiny and public attention athletes experience during their college experience, contemporary Division I athletes often struggle to balance their roles as student and athlete. To this end, college athletes often struggle to intentionally focus on preparation for life after sports due to the sport-specific demands placed upon them during their higher-education experience. This chapter presents empirical data from a qualitative, phenomenological study on the athlete experience in identifying how academic-support centers nested in athletics can better support Division I athletes who garner enhanced media attention in the 21st century. Building on findings from personal narratives, this chapter presents implications for student-affairs practitioners who work to support athletes as they approach the transition to life after sports.

Making the Connection, pages 91–108

INTRODUCTION

Throughout the 21st century, the commercialization of intercollegiate athletics and the subsequent media attention that Division I athletes garner, presents these individuals with a continued struggle to balance their roles as student and athlete (Bell, 2009; Comeaux & Harrison, 2011; Croissant, 2001; Jolly, 2008). To this end, the National Collegiate Athletic Association (NCAA) continues to mandate that contemporary Division I athletic departments must provide general academic counseling and tutoring services for all athletes (NCAA, 2010). The inception of CHAMPS/ Life Skills programs among Division I institutions in 1994 demonstrated a significant shift in policy as the NCAA recognized the need for athletic departments to also provide holistic personal development programs internal to academic support centers (NCAA, 2003). However, while the NCAA clearly continues to delineate specific academic assistance models (e.g., NCAA Academic Progress Rate) for athletes during their four to five-year eligibility window, expectations and learning outcomes for holistic personal development programming continue to emerge in Division I athletic departments. This presents an opportunity for scholars to further probe how student-affairs professionals who work with athletes can best serve both the personal and academic needs of contemporary Division I athletes.

As athletes near the end of their higher-education experience and face the transition to life after sports, contemporary student affairs professionals now often serve dual roles as both academic advisors and career counselors (Chartrand & Lent, 1987; Hill, Burch-Ragan, & Yates, 2001; Wittmer, Bostic, Phillips, & Waters, 1981). Today practitioners who work in athletics' academic support units are often expected to offer support to athletes as they navigate their undergraduate study programs and prepare for life after sports. Advising models to enhance athlete academic success are presented in the student affairs literature (Comeaux & Harrison, 2011). Yet, there is little mention of how intercollegiate athletic departments can better prepare athletes for life after sports via meaningful personal and career development training.

Building on this gap in the literature, this chapter examines the career construction processes of Division I athletes who attend a large, highly selective research institution. The chapter begins with a discussion of current literature delineating the identity development and role-conflict challenges contemporary Division I athletes often face. Following this discussion of current literature, an empirical research study is highlighted to further unpack how contemporary athletes interpret life experiences as student and athlete to prepare for life after sports. Framed from a constructivist epistemology, this phenomenological study considers the life experiences of 29 senior student athletes, who recently completed a formal four-year career development curriculum internal to the athletic department. Semistructured interviews were employed to better understand what life experiences were most salient to these individuals as they prepared for careers after sports. Implications from this empirical study are provided to guide and inform the practices of student-affairs professionals who work with this special population of students. Implications can assist with the development of future athlete personal and career development programs internal to academic-support centers.

BACKGROUND

Throughout the late 1900s and early 21st century, National Collegiate Athletic Association (NCAA) Division I intercollegiate athletic departments have emerged as multimillion dollar operations nested within institutions of higher education (Lapchick, 2006). In turn, this emergence of athletic departments as big-business entities has posed challenges for contemporary student athletes. Today's Division I athlete is placed in challenging position as he or she must balance dual roles as student and athlete (Adler & Adler, 1987; Brewer, Raalte, & Linder, 1993; Harrison et al., 2009; Snyder, 1985). Tension between athletic and academic systems varies across institutions and divisional classifications. However, the experiences of Division I athletes collectively are of heightened interest in 21st century students-affairs literature (Bowen & Levin, 2003; Croissant, 2001). To this end, the sections that follow highlight two specific challenges athletes face with respect to personal and career development processes.

Role Conflict

Bronfenbrenner (1979) defines a role as "a specific set of activities expected of an individual, which are often identified by the use of labels" (p. 85). Adler and Adler (1987), seminal scholars in the area of athlete development, suggest athletes during their undergraduate experience face intense challenges to balance dual roles as student and athlete. In today's higher education system, these individuals are often publicly labeled as athletes first, and students second (Adler & Adler, 1987; Althouse, 2010; Brewer et al., 1993; Broughton & Neyer, 2001; Snyder, 1985). The university expects athletes to perform in the classroom, assuming the primary role of student (Lapchick, 2006). However, demands placed on athletes to perform in the athletic arena often cause these individuals to identify more closely with the role of athlete (Baille & Danish, 1992; Blann, 1985; Miller

& Kerr, 2003; Purdy, Eitzen, & Hufnagel, 1982; Umbach, Palmer, Kuh, & Hannah, 2006). In turn, this tension between the roles of student and athlete throughout the college experience can cloud individual career construction processes. College athletes who fail to recognize the tremendous demands of the athlete role, may encounter enhanced turmoil as graduation and their transition to life after sports draws closer (Meyer, 2003). For many student athletes, the ability to balance and identify with roles as both student and athlete is crucial to career success in life after sports. However, student-affairs professionals still struggle to understand how to best prepare athletes for this transition to life after sports.

Purposeful Engagement

Throughout the current literature base on role conflict, leading scholars (Brewer et al., 1993; Harrison et al., 2009; Settles, Sellers, & Damas, 2002; Snyder, 1985; Yopyk & Prentice, 2005) continue to study how this intricate balance to identify with both student and athlete roles leads to educationally purposeful campus-wide engagement during the undergraduate experience. Astin (1999), Gaston-Gayles and Hu (2009), and Pascarella and Terenzini (2005) suggest that one of the most influential factors in the personal and learning development of students during the college experience is engagement in educationally purposeful activities.

Kuh (2001) discusses how engaging in educationally purposeful activities across the college campus provide both purpose and direction to the undergraduate experience. He argues a student who is purposefully engaged in the undergraduate experience readily invests time in university resources and campus-wide programs, such as interaction with faculty and collaboration with peers in multiple environments. Building on Kuh's (2001) concept of purposeful engagement, researchers must continue to probe just how student athletes, who face these additional internal and external challenges during college, engage purposefully with campus resources to prepare for life after college in career fields (Adler & Adler, 1987; Danish, Petitpas, and Hale, 1993; Gaston-Gayles & Hu, 2009; Miller & Kerr, 2003; Petitpas & Champagne, 1988).

Transition to Life After Sports

Building on the aforementioned struggles that Division I athletes experience in balancing student and athlete roles and engaging in purposeful campus activities, it is no surprise that they often struggle with the transition to life sports (Bell, 2009). According to the NCAA's most recent study on college athletes pursuing professional sports, less than 3% of athletes (on average) who participate in college sport will eventually pursue professional careers in their sport (NCAA, 2011). Regardless of participation in intercollegiate athletics, the transition from college to the real world is often viewed as both difficult and transformational for young adults (Brown, Glastetter-Fender, & Shelton, 2000). Cote (2006) notes that the transition to adulthood is a foundational period of human-identity development. Therefore, additional holistic and personal development support is necessary for athletes to prepare for this life transition. Since athletes may rely to a greater extent on support services internal to athletic departments, it is imperative for student and academic affairs professionals to consider empirical research related to the lived experiences of athletes who approach the transition to life after sports.

METHODOLOGY

To provide student-affairs practitioners with empirical-based research on the athlete experience, this study drew on the epistemological approach of constructivism. Crotty (1998) defines constructivism as a world view in which "all knowledge . . . is contingent upon human practices, being constructed in and out of interaction [with] human beings and their world" (p. 42). This view posits meaning is not discovered, but rather constructed as human beings make meaning from life experiences over the course of their lifespan (Crotty). Moreover, as individuals engage with and experience the world as they know it, they are able to make sense of these lived experiences. Each experience is critical to the collective understanding of a phenomenon.

With this in mind, I asked senior athletes to reflect on their personal experiences as they engaged with campus personal development outlets and support staff to prepare for life after sports in careers. I assumed that the life experiences each individual endured throughout a lifetime would shape the way in which he or she constructed career plans. Further, I drew on the retrospective personal accounts of a cohort of athletes to understand what life experiences during their college experience were most influential as they prepared for career fields.

Theoretical Framework

Crotty (1998) defines a theoretical perspective as "the philosophical stance lying behind a methodology" (p. 66). I framed this study utilizing an overarching interpretivism theoretical framework. Interpretive research uses human interpretation to develop knowledge about a phenomenon (Crotty). Throughout this study I relied on individuals to reflect on and interpret personal life experiences with respect to career preparation processes. Moreover, I drew on Savickas' (2002) interpretive theory of career construction to guide my analysis. Savickas (2002) posits as humans consider vocational alternatives, that life experiences shape career decision-making processes. He argues individuals actively respond to external environmental factors as they engage in career decision making and preparation processes. In turn, career-related decisions are constructed as individuals adapt to specific factors of their external environment and make meaning of these events.

Research Questions

To develop a further understanding of how Savickas's (2002) theory of career construction applies to the athlete population, I developed the following guiding research questions from the perspective of 29 NCAA Division I student athletes:

1. What life experiences influenced these athletes as they explored career alternatives?
2. What life experience influenced these athletes as they chose career fields?
3. What life experiences prepared these athletes for career fields in life after sport?

These three research questions, in addition to Savickas' (2002) theoretical framework, further informed my methodological design.

Research Design

Because this study involved understanding the specific individual interpretations of student-athletes' life experiences to inform career-related decisions, I employed a multiple semistructured individual interview design as the primary method of data collection. To contact athlete participants, I employed a purposeful sampling technique (Patton, 2002). I distributed an initial email message including a written consent form and outline of the study to an email list provided by the Office of Student-Athlete Support Services. This email message extended an invitation to all participants meeting selection criteria. From this recruitment process, 29 students agreed to participate. Demographic information for the study participants appear in Tables 7.1 and 7.2. Participant names were replaced by pseudonyms to ensure anonymity.

Data Collection

Individuals were slotted for 75 min semistructured individual interviews. During each interview session, I distributed a short demographic survey to

TABLE 7.1 Profiles of Male Participants

Pseudonym	Sport	Major	Career Aspiration	Student/Academic Affairs Professional Cited as Influential
Kevin	Football	Sociology	Financial Representative / Business Manager	Athletics
Aaron	Football	International Studies Spanish	Global Security	Athletics and Campus
Darius	Football	Zoology	Physical Therapist	Athletics
Jared	Football	Sociology Religious Studies	Professor of Sociology	Athletics
Jonte	Football	Human Ecology	NFL/Paramedic/ Mentor Program Coordinator	Athletics and Campus
Lamar	Football	Sociology	NFL/ PE Teacher	Athletics
John	Football	History European Studies	Athletic Director	Athletics
Terrance	Football	Human Ecology	NFL/Sport Marketing and PR Representative	Athletics
Jamal	Basketball	Political Science	Coach/Lawyer	Athletics
Dan	Track and Field	Business Management	Sales/PR/Coach	Athletics
Devin	Track and Field	Sociology	Sport Administrator	Athletics
Karl	Track and Field	Sociology	Physical Therapist Assistant	Athletics
Cameron	Swimming	Mechanical Engineering	Engineer	Campus
Taylor	Wrestling	Political Science and Communication Arts	Lawyer	Campus
Zeb	Rowing	Chemistry History of Science	Researcher/ Chemist	Campus
Ben	Tennis	Finance	Financial Analyst	Campus

TABLE 7.2 Profiles of Female Participants

Pseudonym	Sport	Major	Career Aspiration	Student/Academic Affairs Professional Cited as Influential
Joy	Volleyball	Rehabilitation Psychology	Occupational Therapist for Children	Athletics and Campus
Jenny	Volleyball	Human Development	High School Guidance Counselor/Athletics Director	Athletics and Campus
Abby	Volleyball	Elementary Education	Teacher/Athletics Director	Athletics and Campus
Amanda	Volleyball	Human Development	Early Childhood Education/ Athletics Director	Athletics and Campus
Lucy	Soccer	Communications Political Science	Public Relations/ Athletics Director	Athletics and Campus
Anna	Softball	Sociology	Sports Marketing Representative	Athletics
Karla	Track and Field	Consumer Affairs Certificate in Business	Sports Marketing Representative	Athletics
Molly	Cross Country	Elementary Education Anthropology	Teacher, Coach	Athletics and Campus
Rachel	Swimming	Sociology Legal Studies	FBI Agent	Athletics
Amber	Women's Swimming	Human Ecology	HR/Sports Marketing Representative	Athletics
Andrea	Women's Rowing	Sociology and Biology	Optometrist	Campus
Jayne	Women's Tennis	Communication Arts	Athletic Directors	Athletics
Karen	Women's Golf	Human Development	Speech Pathologist/ Child Life Specialist	Campus

begin the session. Using this as a guide, I then employed a semistructured guiding interview protocol to frame each interview. Within this guiding protocol, I asked athletes to recall what life experiences during their higher education experience were most salient to preparation for transition to life after sports. Participants were able to expound upon this question and provide additional information on their experiences with respect to preparation for career fields.

Data Analysis

Following all interviews, I utilized the assistance of a secure transcription service to transcribe all audio files. Final transcripts were sent to participants for approval prior to analysis. Once member checks were completed, I employed three data analysis techniques including process coding, pattern coding, and analytic memoing. In the first round of coding, I employed a process-coding technique to search for ongoing actions, interactions or emotions in response to life experiences as individual discussed their process of narrowing major choice alternatives (Saldaña, 2009). I utilized this form of coding, which assigned action oriented "ing" words to themes, to produce an individual storyline for each participant. From this storyline, I was able to develop a cognitive mind map for each individual that depicted how he or she interpreted the specific life event that influenced preparation for life after sports in a career field. Following this initial coding process, I utilized a pattern-coding technique to recognize themes across individual storylines (Bogdan & Biklen, 2007). This technique enabled me to identify codes across cases and develop collective themes in the data set. These process and pattern codes facilitated the development of a theme-based chart to display trends in data with respect to major choice and alignment of career aspiration.

FINDINGS

Career Preparation

College athletes described six main themes with respect to which college life experiences were influential in preparing them for career fields. The following themes will be outlined: (a) completing a career development course; (b) practicing interviewing skills; (c) attending a resume/cover letter workshop; (d) engaging in networking opportunities; (e) completing a practicum/internship; and (f) being a student athlete. Figure 7.1 provides a visual representation of how these specific themes correlated with perceptions of readiness for life after sports.

Life experiences with respect to career preparation centered around three main themes: (a) completion of activities internal to athletics in the form of a career class; (b) campus and community wide networking and practicum activities; and (c) developing transferrable skillsets as a student athlete. The first three life experiences (e.g., completing a career development course, practicing interview skills, attending a resume/cover letter workshop) all centered on professional development activities completed in the form of a seminar or class setting internal to athletics.

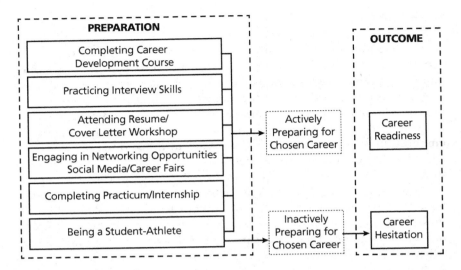

Figure 7.1 Student-athlete career preparation.

The majority of individuals cited these career development class activities as influential in career preparation. Kevin (football) best illustrated this theme when he stated:

> The career-development course I took this year helped me, like, refine all the tools I have, all the skills I have which made me more of, I guess, how to be a better prospect to companies. It was helpful, the fact that you kind of are thinking about how you're gonna go about things when you're done with college and how you're gonna go about getting a job and networking because that's not something that just, I feel like, a lot of kids think about before they graduate. They tend to think about it after, when they need the job, and I think it's a great thing to start thinking about before you graduate.

Similarly, Joy (volleyball) expressed how helpful a career development class in athletics was to her development as she stated:

> The career development course I took this year...my senior year...really helped me to understand the importance of reaching out to people in my field and getting experience. Doing some site visits really helped me to land an internship in a rehab center and make job connections earlier than some of my friends. Since my sport was over, I really could focus on the next step of my life and this class made me realize I couldn't hold off any longer to figure things out. I probably should have even started earlier.

Of specific interest, Joy noted that she would have benefitted from focusing on career development and networking opportunities earlier in her college experience, but time spent with her sport often overshadowed the urgency to do so. Zeb (rowing) shared similar sentiments and stated: "The career course [forced] me come to terms with the fact my time as a student athlete was coming to a close and I had to think about the next phase rather than pretending I wasn't going to move on." Overall students noted an athletic department driven career-development course was beneficial as it required them to intentionally focus on career preparation for life after sports. Many noted that without this course, the amount of time they committed to their sport and studies would have inhibited their ability to intentionally focus on career-development activities.

Further, multiple participants discussed how participation in organized events or professional experiences outside of the classroom setting (e.g., engaging in networking opportunities and completing a practicum or internship) were influential experiences for career preparation. Specific differences were identified with respect to major choice. while business and engineering related majors tended to draw on networking experiences as influential, individuals in education tended to discuss practicum experiences as most influential. Terrance (football) offered,

> I really enjoyed the diversity barbeque where they got all these professionals from the business world to come in and talk to us, and they do pretty well for themselves...just seeing some people that are successful in the business world and connect me helped me the most.

Alternatively, Molly (cross country), an education major stated:

> The best preparation for me for life after I graduate has been our practicums in the classroom. I mean, we have done a lot of great work in theory and stuff, but I think I have grown so much more professionally in the classroom. If you would have asked me before I did my practicum, I would say I was not ready and scared to death to teach. Now I can say I'm ready.

While the majority of students discussed the importance of gaining real world experience and connections in their aspired field, the desired forum to gain this real world experience differed based upon the participant's undergraduate major and field.

Finally, of particular interest to this study, all participants discussed a common interpretation that being an athlete best prepared them for success in career fields with respect to transferrable skills. Amber (swimming) provided an interpretation of how perseverance in sport prepared her for a career in marketing. She offered:

> I think that any job is like swimming. You are going to start out at the bottom and then you just have to prove to people that you can do more and you can

be more successful...it's like if we have a couple of relay spots open and
there may only be a spot for one person. Learning to step up...that will be
helpful in the workplace.

In addition, participants who represented team sports discussed how
working with others in a team setting best prepared them for careers. Jared
(football) offered:

Just this whole college process and being part of this football team that requires a lot of discipline and time management has prepared me for the real
world.... But I think the team part definitely shaped me for being successful.
A career is kind of like just another whole continuation of football camaraderie and teamwork.

While all athletes cited their life experiences of being an athlete as influential to preparing for careers, how they viewed this differed. Individuals who
participated in team sports, specifically men's football, cited the team aspect
of sport as influential to success in career fields. However, participants who
represented individual sports such as swimming tended to discuss perseverance and adaptability as critical success factors for career fields.

DISCUSSION

Today members of the American labor force face additional challenges to
not only find and sustain jobs, but also to develop lifelong careers during
a time of economic instability (Savickas, 2002, 2005). In turn, individuals
must place a greater emphasis on intentionally preparing for meaningful,
long-term careers in a highly competitive job market (Savickas et al., 2009).
To this end, this study specifically focused on how student athletes, a specific subset of the larger student body in higher education, navigate the
processes of career exploration, choice, and preparation while balancing
roles as student and athlete.

Reliance on the College Athlete Experience

Previous literature addresses how athletes often struggle to balance
roles as student and athlete during the college experience (Adler & Adler,
1987; Althouse, 2010; Brewer et al., 1993; Broughton & Neyer, 2001; Snyder, 1985). Findings from this study provide a unique interpretation of how
athletes balance dual roles. Interestingly, results from this study suggest
participants widely regard their experience balancing roles as both student
and athlete as significant preparation for future career fields. In particular,

participants felt consistently balancing dual roles as student and athlete prepared them for a multifaceted and fast-paced career. However, student-affairs practitioners should interpret these results with caution. If athletes rely solely on transferrable skills obtained during their college experience, this may present challenges to career development. For example, athletes who only depend on skills developed during college may fail to intentionally engage in other crucial career development preparation tasks such as resume development, cover letter development, and networking with individuals in their aspired field. Student affairs practitioners should assist athletes in understanding that preparation for life after sports is an intentional process that requires both time and effort. While students seem to view skillsets to multitask and overcome adversity learned as an athlete as beneficial, student-affairs practitioners must continue to instill structured career and personal development programming that enables athletes to intentionally focus on other aspects of career development. In this study, participants noted that their ability to intentionally focus on career preparation activities such as completing reflective self-assessments, networking with potential employers via social media, developing job search documents, and completing exploratory site visits enabled them to better cope with the impending transition to life after sports. They further discussed their appreciation of a focus on such tasks in a classroom setting and outside of the public eye.

Importance of Purposeful Engagement to Career Construction Processes

Kuh (2001) and Gaston-Gayles and Hu (2009) discuss the importance of student engagement (e.g., investing time with peer, faculty, and support staff across campus) in fostering positive career outcomes in life after the higher-education experience. The conceptual model of athlete career preparation processes developed from this empirical study suggests athletes continue to struggle to engage with their campus. Participant narratives suggest Division I athletes continue to rely heavily on athletics-specific personnel and support programs throughout college to choose and prepare for career fields. Of specific interest, these narratives illustrate athletes often rely on support systems within their athletics environment more readily than campus-based support systems. This reliance on athletics support services can often inhibit holistic career construction processes and campus-wide engagement as athletes often more readily seek out individuals that can relate to their role as an athlete. In turn, it is paramount for athletic personnel to continue to explore how to incorporate integrative campus support systems early in the college experience to facilitate successful postcollege career outcomes. More specifically, findings agree with previous literature (Bell, 2009; Comeaux & Harrison, 2011; Harrison & Lawrence, 2003; Sowa & Gressard, 1983) that state it is important for athletics and campus-based student support personnel to recognize, foster, and support both student and athlete roles. Enhanced support of both athletics and academic responsibilities campus wide will not only lessen role tension, but will also promote successful transitions to life after college and intercollegiate athletic participation.

IMPLICATIONS FOR PRACTITIONERS

Implications for Policy

Over time, the NCAA has attempted to require member institutions to more intentionally prepare Division I athletes for life after sports via life-skills programs. In 1994, this organization first issued a mandate that required all Division I athletic departments to support and sustain holistic academic, career, and personal training (i.e., CHAMPS/Life Skills programming). In theory, each Division I college campus is now required to provide some form of personal and career development programming for athletes in addition to academic support. However, this NCAA policy continues to exist today without specific benchmarks or desired learning objectives (NCAA, 2003).

In 2010, the NCAA developed a division of student athlete affairs to consider additional reform. However, even with this recent restructuring, career development programs internal to athletics continue to exist without national regulation or assessment. Therefore, campus-level athletic administrators must work to ensure programs do not simply exacerbate tensions between academic and athletic systems, but enable athletes to intentionally prepare for meaningful career paths. Building on Comeaux's (2013) work that encourages organizational innovation in athlete academic support services, collaboration must continue between NCAA athlete-welfare officials and campus-based athletics student-support personnel. This collaboration is necessary to develop clear program learning objectives and assessment measures at both the national and campus levels. It is imperative that policy makers at both the national and campus levels consider the athlete voice as they craft programmatic initiatives and benchmarks.

Implications for Practice

Empirical findings from this study can be useful to student-affairs professionals as they continue to work to support the personal and career development of Division I athletes. Moving forward, student-affairs professionals who work closely with athletes should consider the importance of research and how it can be used to inform decision making about the athlete experience. As such, a data-driven approach on the athlete experience may assist contemporary student-affairs practitioners in developing intentional programs that better prepare students for the transition to life after sports.

Building on the notion of a data-driven approach in academic support centers, this study demonstrated athletes often draw on life experiences salient to their role as an athlete when preparing for career fields. However, this finding is problematic as very few participants discussed academic support units as adequately facilitating holistic and intentional career development programming over the course of the entire college experience. Three main suggestions are presented for practitioners.

First, many athletes noted that career programming was most intensified during the senior year, but that this was often too late in their higher-education experience. Therefore, it is suggested that athletic practitioners work to provide career programming throughout the four-year experience so athletes will begin to understand the importance of preparing for the transition to life after sports at different times.

Second, findings suggest the athletes' sense of urgency to prepare for this transition appears to be further complicated as athletics responsibilities often take precedence over personal and career development. In turn, practitioners may benefit from making select career development programming mandatory for athletes to ensure some focus is given to this area amid other role expectations.

Third, given the importance of intentional focus on career preparation for this population, practitioners who work with athlete populations must work to achieve a stronger balance between athletic-specific and campus-wide career development initiatives. As intercollegiate athletic practitioners seek to incorporate evidence-based seminars, courses, and workshops into athletes' weekly routines, they should consider the athletes' voice to determine how time can be best spent. Moreover, findings from this study suggest that confining athletes solely to athletic-specific programming may inhibit networking opportunities and long-term career preparation. Moving forward, athletic practitioners may seek to engage in intentional professional development activities with both campus-wide student affairs professionals and potential employers to better serve athletes as they prepare for life after sports.

QUESTIONS FOR DISCUSSION

1. Consider the location of career programming on your current campus. In what ways may this influence one's ability to balance student and athlete roles?

2. Given the multiple roles of student support staff, how might practitioners balance the delivery of academic advising and career development training for athletes on your campus?
3. This chapter notes recommendations for practitioners to continue to shape holistic career development programs for student-athletes. How would you suggest athlete support staff develop and implement a multiyear career development program for athletes?
4. Considering this multiyear plan, how might you incorporate campus-based career development assistance? What challenges might this multiyear plan pose for athletes?
5. Considering this multiyear plan, how might you work with future employers to provide career development assistance to current student athletes? What challenges might you experience in doing so?
6. Savickas suggests career development is a multifaceted process in which individuals adapt and learn from salient life experiences as they craft career plans. How might tension between both roles as student and athlete further implicate career preparation for Division I athletes?

REFERENCES

Astin, A. W. (1999). Student involvement: A developmental theory for higher education. *Journal of College Student Development, 40*(5), 518–529.

Althouse, J. N. (2007). *Testing a model of first-semester student-athlete academic motivation and motivational balance between academics and athletics* (Doctoral dissertation, The Pennsylvania State University).

Adler, P., & Adler, P. (1987). Role conflict and identity salience: College athletics and the academic role. *Social Science Journal 24,* 443–450.

Baille, P. H., & Danish, S. J. (1992). Understanding the career transition of athletes. *The Sport Psychologist, 6,* 77–98

Bell, L. F. (2009). Examining academic role-set influence on the student-athlete experience. *Journal of Issues in Intercollegiate Athletics, 19*(4), 19–41.

Blann, F. W. (1985). Intercollegiate athletic competition and students' educational and career plans. *Journal of College Student Personnel, 26*(2), 115–118.

Bogdan, R. C., & Biklen, S. K. (2007). *Qualitative research for education: An introduction to theories and methods* (5th ed.). Boston, MA: Pearson.

Bowen, W.G., & Levin, S.A. (2003). *Reclaiming the game: College sports and educational values.* Princeton, NJ: Princeton University Press.

Brewer, B. W., Van Raalte, J. L., & Linder, D. E. (1993). Athletic identity: Hercules' muscle or Achilles heel? *International Journal of Sport Psychology, 24,* 237–254.

Bronfenbrenner, U. (1979). *The ecology of human development.* Cambridge, MA: Harvard University Press.

Broughton, E., & Neyer, M. (2001). Advising and counseling student athletes. *New Directions for Student Services, 93,* 47–53.

Brown, C., Glastetter-Fender, C., & Shelton, M. (2000). Psychosocial identity and career control in college student athletes. *Journal of Vocational Behavior, 56,* 53–62.

Chartrand, J. M., & Lent, R. W. (1987). Sports counseling: Enhancing the development of the student athlete. *Journal of Counseling and Development, 66*(4), 164–167.

Comeaux, E. (2013). Rethinking academic reform and encouraging organizational innovation: Implications for stakeholder management in college sports. *Innovative Higher Education, 38,* 281–293.

Comeaux, E., & Harrison, C. K. (2011). A conceptual model of academic success for student athletes. *Educational Researcher, 40,* 235–245.

Cote, J. E. (2006). Emerging adulthood as an institutionalized moratorium: Risks and benefits to identity formation. In J. J. Arnett & J. L. Tanner (Eds.), *Emerging adults in America: Coming of age in the 21st century* (pp. 85–116). Washington, DC: American Psychological Association.

Croissant, J. L. (2001). Can this campus be bought? Commercial influence in unfamiliar places. *Academe 87*(5), 44–48.

Crotty, M. (2010). *The foundations of social research: Meaning and perspective in the research process.* Thousand Oaks, CA: Sage.

Danish, S. J., Petitpas, A. J., & Hale, B. D. (1993). Life development intervention for athletes: Life skills through sports. *Counseling Psychologist, 21,* 352–385.

Gaston Gayles, J., & Hu, S. (2009). The influence of student engagement and sport participation on college outcomes among Division I student athletes. *Journal of Higher Education, 80*(3), 315–333.

Harrison, C. K., & Lawrence, S. M. (2003). African-American student athletes' perceptions of career transition in sport: A qualitative and visual elicitation. *Race, Ethnicity and Education, 6,* 373–394.

Harrison, C. K., Stone, J., Shapiro, J., Yee, S., Boyd, J. A., & Rullan, V. (2009). The role of gender identities and stereotype salience with the academic performance of male and female college athletes. *Journal of Sport & Social Issues, 33*(1), 78–96.

Hill, K., Burch-Ragan, K., & Yates, D. Y. (2001). Current and future issues and trends facing student athletes and athletic programs. *New Directions for Student Services, 93,* 65–80.

Jolly, J. C. (2008). Raising the question #9: Is the student-athlete population unique, and why should we care? *Communication Education, 57*(1), 145–151.

Kuh, G. D. (2001). Assessing what really matters to student learning: Inside the National Survey of Student Engagement. *Change, 33*(3), 10–17.

Lapchick, R. E. (2006). *New game plan for college sport.* Westport, CT: Praeger.

Meyer, K. J. (2003). *Influences on career decisions of college student athletes.* [Unpublished master's thesis]. Northwestern University, Evanston, IL.

Miller, P. S., & Kerr, G. A. (2003). The role experimentation of intercollegiate student athletes. *The Sport Psychologist, 17,* 196–219.

National Collegiate Athletic Association. (2003). "CHAMPS/life skills program." Retrieved from http://www.ncaa.org/wps/ncaa?key=/ncaa/NCAA/Academics+and+Athletes

National Collegiate Athletic Association. (2010). *2010-11 NCAA Division I manual: Constitutional operating bylaws, administrative bylaws*, [Effective August 1, 2010]. Indianapolis, IN: NCAA.

National Collegiate Athletic Association. (2011). "Estimated probability of competing in athletics beyond the high-school interscholastic level." Retrieved from http://www.ncaa.org/wps/wcm/connect/public/NCAA/Issues/Recruiting/Probability+of+Going+Pro

Pascarella, E. T., & Terenzini, P. T. (2005). *How college affects students* (Vol. 2). K. A. Feldman (Ed.). San Francisco, CA: Jossey-Bass.

Patton, M. Q. (2002). *Qualitative research & evaluation methods.* (3rd. ed.), Thousand Oaks, CA: Sage.

Petitpas, A. J., & Champagne, D. E. (1988). Developmental programming for intercollegiate athletes. *Journal of College Student Development, 29,* 454–460.

Purdy, D. A., Eitzen, D. S., & Hufnagel, R. (1982). Are athletes also students? The educational attainment of college athletes. *Social Problems, 29,* 439–448.

Saldaña, J. (2009). *The coding manual for qualitative researchers.* Thousand Oaks, CA: Sage.

Savickas, M. L. (2002). Career construction: A developmental theory of vocational behavior. In D. Brown & Associates (Eds.), *Career choice and development* (4th ed., pp. 149–205). San Francisco, CA: Jossey-Bass.

Savickas. M. L. (2005). The theory and practice of career construction. In S. D. Brown & R. W. Lent (Eds.), *Career development and counseling: Putting theory and research to work* (pp. 42–70). Hoboken, NJ: Wiley.

Savickas, M. L., Nota, L., Rossier, J., Dauwalder, J. P., Duarte, M. E., Guichard, J., Salvatore, S., Van Esbroeck, R., & Van Vianen, A. E. (2009). Life designing: A paradigm for career construction in the 21st century, *Journal of Vocational Behavior, 75,* 239–250.

Settles, I. H., Sellers, R. M., & Damas, A., Jr. (2002). One role or two? The function of psychological separation in role conflict. *Journal of Applied Psychology, 87,* 574–582.

Snyder, E. E. (1985). A theoretical analysis of academic and athletic roles. *Sociology of Sport Journal, 2,* 210–217.

Sowa, C., & Gressard, C. (1983). Athletic participation: Its relationship to student development. *Journal of College Student Personnel, 24,* 236–239.

Umbach, P. D., Palmer, M. M., Kuh, G. D., & Hannah, S. J. (2006). Intercollegiate athletes and effective educational practices: Winning combination or losing effort? *Research in Higher Education, 47,* 709. doi:10.2307/40197573

Wittmer, J., Bostic, D., Phillips, T. D., & Waters, W. (1981). The personal, academic, and career problems of college student athletes: Some possible answers. *Personnel and Guidance Journal, 60*(1), 52–55.

Yopyk, D. J. A., & Prentice, D. A. (2005). Am I an athlete or a student? Identity salience and stereotype threat in student athletes. *Basic & Applied Social Psychology, 27,* 329–336. doi:10.1207/s15324834basp2704_5

CHAPTER 8

BRIDGING THE GAP

Academic Support for Entering Special-Admit College Athletes

Anne Browning

ABSTRACT

Drawing from a four-week writing intensive course through a Summer Bridge Program (Bridge) for Division I special-admit athletes (athletes with low academic profiles), this chapter examines the impact of this academic-skills intervention on the academic performance of these athletes. Through participant observation and interviews with seven football players and two Bridge staff members, the qualitative data demonstrated the value of academic centers operating as a *hybrid space* between athletics and academics, expanding what counts as competent participation, and allowing for points of entry into difficult academic material. The findings also revealed the challenge for practitioners to navigate the historic storylines of figurative identities and the subsequent low position of special-admit athletes within the academic domain.

Making the Connection, pages 109–123

INTRODUCTION

The American higher education system is unique for its intertwining of athletics into its academic institutions. Over the last century, intercollegiate athletics has grown into a massive commercialized enterprise, one that some scholars fear threatens the university systems' core academic values (Shulman & Bowen, 2001). Colleges are pressured to field the most competitive teams possible, even if athletic competition falls outside of the school's stated mission (Clodfelter, 2011). While many low-profile sports, often referred to as Olympic sports, avoid the limelight until there are brief glimpses of campus celebrities during championship seasons, men's basketball, football, and (in some leagues) men's ice hockey are the focus of both the campus sporting culture and potential streams of revenue for athletic departments. Football and men's basketball are often referred to as revenue-generating sports, but due to the reality that only a handful of teams, even in Division 1 athletics, generate enough revenue to cover their actual operating costs, I will refer to teams that are the focus of campus culture and media attention as high-profile sports (Shulman & Bowen, 2001).[1] In order to win more games, especially in high-profile sports, colleges and universities lower their academic standards and admit applicants who they bet will make contributions on the playing field, but whose academic profiles are out of step with their classmates (Bowen & Levin, 2003).

As a result, the National Collegiate Athletic Association (NCAA) reacted to the shifting landscape of intercollegiate athletics by enacting mandates for academic support. In 1991, the NCAA established bylaw 16.3.1.1, which requires athletic departments to provide academic counseling and tutoring for all recruited athletes. The NCAA points to subsequent improvements in the graduation success rate of college athletes (currently over 80%) as proof that academic reform and mandated support is working. But Bowen and Levin (2003) point out that while graduation rates are steady or improving, athletes' rank-in-class positions are declining, indicating a growing divide between athletes and students at large. Ultimately, the academic counseling and tutoring of athletes is often negatively viewed as an "eligibility game" in which advisers and counselors navigate NCAA policy and the athlete's academic proficiency to help maintain his or her progress towards a degree (North Carolina, 2012).

THE CASE OF THE SPECIAL ADMIT

There is no universally-used term for athletes who are admitted and enrolled with low academic profiles, but the most common is *special admit* (Jaschik, 2008). While some institutions determine special-admit status through the use of a complex equation combining the applicant's high school GPA and SAT/ACT scores to predict his or her likelihood of holding at least a 2.0 GPA at the end of the student's first year of college, the common definition can be reduced to "students admitted under exceptions to normal admissions standards for reasons including 'special talent'" (Alesia, 2008). Journalists at *The Indianapolis Star* newspaper compiled data on special admits from 55 public institutions, of which 31 admitted to having special admits (Alesia, 2008). What journalists and researchers found most significant from the study was the discrepancy between the percentage of football players enrolled as special admits and the percentage of students at large enrolled as special admits. In 2004, the University of California at Berkeley reported that 95% of its freshman football players were special admits, compared with 2% of the students at large (Jaschik, 2008).

The purpose of this chapter is to observe special-admit Division I athletes' negotiation of athletic and academic domains from within the system of institutional support at their point of entry into the university. Specifically, drawing from a four-week writing intensive course through a Summer Bridge Program (Bridge) for special-admit athletes, this chapter seeks to understand how this academic-skills intervention by personnel in academic support services impacts the students' ability to navigate the academic world of the university. Bridge, the studied university's nationally acclaimed program, was developed using a data-driven approach primarily for the development and retention of special-admit athletes. Bridge also represents a novel attempt to mitigate the academic preparation gap for special admits before they arrive on campus for their first year, through the program's stated goals: helping athletes acquire study skills and habits, immerse them into academic culture, and prepare them for writing composition.

The following questions guide this research study:

1. What do college athletes learn in Bridge?
2. What counts as competent participation in the hybrid space of Bridge?
3. What figurative and positional identities do college athletes adopt and create?

INFORMING LITERATURE

Although access to the academic domain of the university is granted with admission, in reality, access is effectively limited by athletes' status as *dumb jocks*. Sociologist Harry Edwards (1984) describes the codification of the college athlete as athletically superior and academically deficient, and that "dumb jocks are not born; they are systematically created" (p. 8). Bowen and Levin (2003) critique the opportunity cost associated with admitting college athletes with lower than average incoming SAT scores and high-school grade point averages, especially in light of researchers' findings that college athletes as a whole academically underperform below what their incoming credentials predict. The underperformance observed by Bowen and Levin is seen most severely among athletes participating in high-profile sports (Maloney & McCormick, 1991) and Black male athletes (Umbach, Kuh & Hannah, 2006). Because of NCAA mandates for support and sanctions for failing to keep athletes on a path toward a degree, one would expect the support to boost athletes' performance relative to their peers. However, research finds that the opposite effect is true: special admits are underperforming despite institutional support (Shulman & Bowen, 2001). Researchers have quantitatively looked at athletes' academic performance as connected to stigma (Simons, Bosworth, Jensen, & Fujita, 2007), stereotype threat (Stone, Harrison & Mottley, 2012), and cognitive versus non-cognitive variables (Hyatt, 2003). Qualitative research has focused on issues of athletic role engulfment and pragmatic detachment (Adler & Adler, 1985, 1991) and has been leveraged to challenge deficit perspectives of athlete academic underperformance (Benson, 2000).

FIGURED WORLDS AND HYBRID SPACES

The environments athletes experience at college are embedded within a complex structure that includes regulation from an outside governing body, the NCAA (see Figure 8.1).

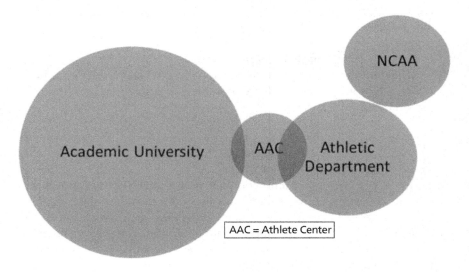

Figure 8.1 The complexity of the system.

However, athletes do not experience college in terms of reporting lines and regulations. They experience worlds in which they have different roles and are met with different expectations. The world of their sport collides and sometimes overlaps with their academic worlds; such worlds are not cleanly defined and contained. The lines separating the worlds blur when an athlete winces in a morning class, or is distracted because his hands are cut and raw from doing "bear crawls" on concrete during early morning football practice. The physical and mental effects of participation in one domain spill over into the next. Figure 8.2 below shows how the systems above are experienced by athletes.

I will use the framework of Figured Worlds[2] to explore how meaning is created and how roles and identities are formed within the spheres athletes inhabit. Figured Worlds are cultural realms in which values, meaning, and identities are constructed by the contexts and actors, and collectively realized within the domain *as if* the collective vision is reality (Holland, 2010). Figured Worlds are shaped by their own unique culture; what anthropologist Clifford Geertz (1973) would frame as *webs of meaning* that hold together the actions of the actors within the culture. Figured Worlds develop out of sociocultural foundations that have matured into what James Greeno (2006) frames as a *situative approach*, which is defined by a shift away from focusing on the individual as the main unit of analysis, and instead focuses on analysis systems (Nolen et al., 2008). Understanding athletes' learning

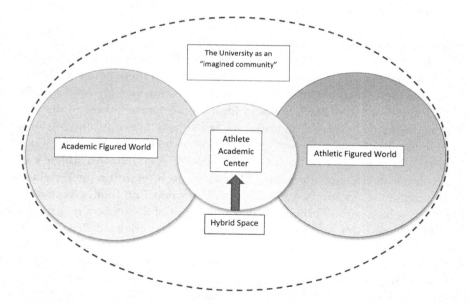

Figure 8.2 Activity systems as experienced in figured worlds.

from a situated perspective necessitates an understanding of the complexity of the social organizations that shape learning. For example, it is important to understand college athletes' interactions with coaches, peers, advisers, learning specialists, faculty, tutors, and the NCAA within such organizations as well as the environments in which interactions take place (Greeno).

Figure 8.2 includes a separate sphere for academic support as an entity overlapping both with athletics and academics, effectively functioning as a bridge between the two worlds for the athletes. As a bridge between worlds, the study center can be described as a hybrid space. Hybrid or third spaces represent flexible zones of proximal development that accept the counter script—student behaviors and learning that might not be accepted in formal Figured Worlds (Gutierrez, Baquedano-Lopez & Tejeda 1999). While Gutierrez and colleagues present the concept of the hybrid space as a method for students to connect unofficial spaces (e.g., home life) with formal spaces (e.g., classrooms) this chapter analyzes academic support centers for athletes as hybrid spaces connecting two formal Figured Worlds. The acceptance of the counter script within the hybrid space allows an athlete access to the domain of academic content without having the same background knowledge base as his or her peers within the academic Figured World.

Holland, Lachicotte, Skinner, & Cain (1998) identify two types of identities that subjects inhabit within Figured Worlds: figurative and positional identities. Figurative identities are "about signs that evoke storylines or plots among generic characters," which for the athlete arriving on campus translate into the often used tropes of the *jock, dumb jock, meat head, football player, baller,* and the less charged, but by no means benign *student athlete* (Holland, p. 128). The historical storylines of these figurative identities function to constrain athletes' (and disproportionately academically underprepared and Black males in high-profile sports) access to the academic domain. Positional identities are "about acts that constitute relations of hierarchy, distance, or perhaps affiliation," which translate into notions of relative power and ability for athletes (Holland, p. 128). An athlete's affiliation with athletics affects his or her social position within the imagined community of the university.[3] Certain athletes may find themselves with a relatively high social position in certain contexts of the university (e.g., the field of play, gyms, dorm space) but they may experience a lower social position within the Figured World of academics (e.g., lectures, seminars, libraries) (Simons et al., 2007). I followed athletes from their point of entry into the universities to look at whether and how the day-to-day interactions around academic support centers lead athletes to form positional identities, and significantly, whether those identities were accepted or rejected.

METHODS

This research offers a look into the systems operating to facilitate and constrain special admits' access to the academic domain. Observations took place at a large, public Division 1 Football Bowl Subdivision (FBS) university in the western United States during a four-week Bridge program in the summer of 2012, during which time Bridge served 41 athletes (26 male, 15 female). Since all entering football players were required to attend Bridge, they made up the majority (58%) of participants. Observations were made at the morning English classes held in an academic building and at an afternoon general studies class held in the academic center supported by tutors and staff. My participant observations were made working in groups and one-on-one with athletes in the role of a tutor. I utilized a grounded-theory approach (Charmaz, 1995) for my participant observations and I triangulated my data (Bloor, 1997) through semistructured interviews with critical-case athletes and staff at the academic support center. I introduced my research and invited all Bridge students to participate during an afternoon class session. I purposively selected all high-profile athletes who volunteered to be interviewed in my sample. As a result, I interviewed seven football players and two full-time professional staff members[4] employed in the center. I used a sequential interviewing technique in which each interview informed the next with the goal of saturation of themes (Small, 2009). Including staff and athlete interviews allowed for a multivoiced triangulation of the observation data. Interviews took place several weeks after Bridge finished and before fall classes began. The seven athletes interviewed were all attending the university from out of state and cited the football program and their connection with the coaches as their primary reason for choosing to attend the university. The athletes were all special admits, but felt they had very different levels of preparation. On one end, Brady characterized his high school as rife with "violence...gangs, drugs, and that stuff." His options were to "do football or...do bad." In contrast, Clayton came from the top high school in his home state. Ultimately, all seven interviewed said that they had learned things in Bridge and felt more prepared as a result.

FINDINGS AND DISCUSSION

Using Charmaz's model of grounded theory, I analyzed my data and developed memoranda during the data-collection phase. As a result of the analysis, four dominant themes emerged: the functions of Bridge as a hybrid space; figurative and positional identities of athletes; entry into the *real* academic domain with the *normies*; and a reconceptualization of the position of the academic support services over time.

Competent Participation in a Hybrid Space

During a tutor-lead small group session in the morning class, the athletes discussed an article on street smarts and academia. Everyone took turns sharing a main idea from the passage and the evidence connected to it. A football player who initially appeared shy and reserved, became animated when he brought the hip hop artist The Notorious B.I.G. into the conversation, telling the other students that Biggie Smalls did not like school, but that "he sounds smart [and has] street smarts and the ability to write poetry." The tutor then used the student's contribution to talk about how the main point develops in the article, and asked the group if they thought the author was trying to sell something. The football player replied, quoting song lyrics and discussing rap culture before catching himself and saying "[I] don't think it has anything to do with the story but..." The tutor then offered the connection: "education is a hustle." The interaction allowed the student to bring the course material in line with his frame of reference: Biggie Smalls and rap. Even though he got a bit lost in his tangent, the tutor was able to help him connect his understanding of street smarts with the author's main argument. The expanded notion of what counts as competent participation within Bridge allowed students to utilize their lived experience to find points of entry into the academic material. Tutors and instructors encouraged the use of students' empirical evidence to draw connections with the author's main points. As a result, dense readings began to carry meaning in the students' day-to-day life.

Beyond the curriculum functioning as a hybrid space linking the informal lived experience and the formal academic domain, tutors and instructors made academia more accessible through the use of language. One set of instructors cursed frequently in front of the class to break with the formality of the space. The students responded favorably to the expanded use of language in an academic setting, showing that instructor relatability was a means of accessing a formal space.

In another instance, a tutor leading a reading group asked a student what he thought of a paragraph he just read aloud. The student replied that the actions of a person in the paragraph represented a "dick move." Without missing a beat, the tutor responded, "Good. I am writing 'dick move' in the margin next to that section." The expansion of valued participation along with encouragement allowed students to take more risks. In a one-on-one tutoring session, a football player sat frozen in front of a blank computer screen and confessed to a tutor that, "I don't know big words." The tutor replied, "You don't need big words—this is rough draft time." The encouragement helped the student begin the daunting task of starting his close reading essay. Later, the tutor continued working with the student suggesting that he try to use Freire's language and "instead of using 'messed up' use 'oppressed'." The tutor used the student's informal language and helped to translate it into the formal language of academia, but the tutor did not allow the initial inability to write using academic terminology to deter the student from getting out his thoughts.

Broadly, Bridge classrooms were places of high expectations and expanded acceptance of behavior as long as the action served academic goals. Sleeping students were roused and off-task students were nudged back into line, but walking across the classroom to point out an important passage to a friend was acceptable. To avoid creating oppositional behavior in the class, students' comments that were not made in support of academic goals were ignored, but not reprimanded. Ultimately, a strength of Bridge was its ability to allow points of entry into difficult material.

Figurative and Positional Identities

While the English-based content in Bridge helps athletes close the gap in their academic preparation for the university, less overt lessons that are not built into the syllabi of classrooms teach athletes what is expected of them and what roles they will be afforded. As one instructor announced in the afternoon class, "You don't start with a blank slate as a student athlete." Rather, the athletes learn that, "You will be judged . . . where you sit . . . what you wear," and that they will be "held to a different standard" because they are "known." Bridge becomes a point of entry to the university in which athletes can begin to choose which figurative identities to adopt and which to reject, but context itself (the classes, instructors, coaches, and peers) helps educate athletes on the historical caricatures. In revealing the reporting lines between the academic support center and the athletic domain dominated by coaches, one instructor said, "Your coaches ask us who are the sleepers, the leaders, the knuckle heads. . . . They want to get a read on you guys." From this comment, athletes learned what figurative identities are recognized by the staff and coaches they work with, and that there are strong lines of communication between the athletic domain and the academic support center. Further, athletes learned that academic issues were reported to coaches and often resulted in physical punishments blurring the lines between the worlds.

In contrast to figurative identities, positional identities establish power dynamics within specific contexts (Holland et. al., 1998). Because high-profile sports are traditionally played by men, the university uses the vast majority of its special admits on male athletes with the occasional female special admit in a low-profile sport, who can act as a game changer for a team. While Bridge intentionally has a mix of male and female students because, as Lina notes, "women really contribute well in that sense in helping... pushing the guys to participate." Because so few women are brought in as special admits, the dynamic at Bridge teaches athletes that on the whole, females are much more prepared and academically driven than males. Lina was concerned that the lack of many male participants in discussions stemmed from being "scared" and not wanting to "seem dumb" or "say the wrong thing." The difference in positional power held by men and women in Bridge was reflected in the figurative identities they adopted (see Figure 8.3).

Women who were the model students exhibited ideal classroom behavior and responded to instructors' questions. The helpers supported men who fell into the silent and struggling category, acting as peer tutors. The bored and disengaged women saw Bridge as remedial and were resentful of their attendance. Passively resistant men increased in number over time, exhibiting minimal effort even when they were relatively well prepared. As one such male told me, "If I pass, I'm happy." The silent and struggling men were made up of several special admits who were willing to talk with tutors, but not in class where the stakes were higher and they feared appearing underprepared. The quiet and well-prepared group consisted of the men who were not special admits, but who limited their own presentation of their academic skill level within the class so as to avoid standing out relative to other men. Lastly, the charmer established a near-flirtatious relationship with some tutors and staff in which the player used sweetness to elicit support, get out of trouble, or avoid requirements, which allowed for increased support without academic ability being a factor in the discussion. The charmer identity allowed special admits to protect their academic egos.

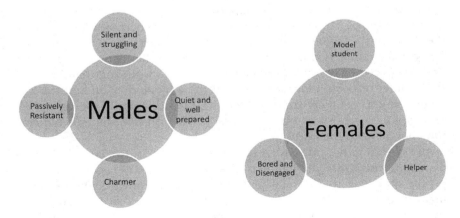

Figure 8.3   Male and female figurative identities.

Identities in Transition to the Academic Figured World

Three-quarters of the way through Bridge, the class attended the university's general new-student orientation program. Orientation was framed as "a chance to meet other students—the normies," the affectionate name for students at large used in the study center. Students were instructed not to "feed into the stereotypes. Show how awake and smart you are." Entering the large auditorium in the center of campus for orientation, the Bridge group sat together in the back. The ways in which athletes chose to be vocal during orientation provided insight into identity formation within the academic Figured World. During a slide show in which the presenter asked students to identify images on the screen, one male who had been quiet during Bridge yelled out responses aggressively. One athlete said, "The regular people don't know us," and another added "they gonna love us." While dominating the participation at orientation, athletes added a layer of self-critique to one another's responses. When one football player attempted an answer but stumbled grammatically, a teammate chimed in, "He's, like, a caveman." A female athlete also stumbled through a response, which earned laughter and the comment, "You must play a sport." When the presenter flashed the number "800+" indicating the number of clubs at the university, one football player shouted, "What I got on my SAT." With the rest of the crowd virtually silent, the college athletes from Bridge stereotyped each other playing into the stigma of athletics and possibly providing a preemptive strike against what they anticipated experiencing walking into a 300-person lecture hall.

Changing Perceptions of Bridge Over Time

Athletes entered Bridge ready to embrace the challenge of their first college course and entry into the academic world. Angela articulated the purpose of Bridge as getting athletes to "see themselves as students," to say, "I think I can do school." The combination of challenging material and support from tutors led to transformative experiences. One football player remarked, "I've never read like this before." Another stated, "I've learned more in the past week than I did in all of high school." Instructors framed the challenge as an academic "boot camp": "We push you, not to put you down, but to pick you up." However, this enthusiasm was not sustained over the summer.

By the end of Bridge, students viewed the course and support as embedded within an athletic domain, as preparation for the type of support they would receive over the year. Instructors framed Bridge as "practice for class" and encouraged athletes to "make mistakes with us" so they could be minimized or avoided later. Significantly, the rhetoric of the instructors shifted to lectures on what *real* college is like. One instructor informed the athletes, "If you mess up something simple, your professor will think you are lazy." In testing situations, "If your phone comes out, they will tell you to leave and they will fail you." In response, Rob felt that, "You were just holding our hands through the whole process; you didn't set us loose and learn by ourselves like college students do." Rob's comment is significant in that it shows how Bridge accentuated the divide between athletes and students at large.

CONCLUSION

Special-admit athletes are recruited heavily into the athletic world at the university. The academic support center functions as a hybrid space to help students pivot between the balanced roles of student and athlete, allowing them access into a world their positional identities might otherwise prevent them from joining. Within Bridge specifically, special admits were granted access to the academic domain by tutors and instructors, who valued their participation and expanded the notion of what counts as competent participation beyond the normal bounds at the university. While Bridge is presented to the students as an opportunity to take risks and make mistakes, the students also learn about the figured identities available to athletes and their relative positions within the community of learners in the academic Figured World. Bridge provided students with essential skills to succeed in the academic domain, but the athletes did not see Bridge as *real* college. Rather than seeing themselves as succeeding in the academic domain through their experiences during Bridge, athletes felt that Bridge trained them on how to work with tutors and utilize support. Relative to the stated goals of Bridge, the actual outcome was an immersion into the work of the hybrid space of the academic center. The question remains as to whether the special-admit students who found their voice valued in Bridge would find such a positive reception in other areas of the academic Figured World.

The themes emerging from the Bridge program data highlight some unintended consequences of current practices by practitioners supporting athletes. Specifically, practitioners should be aware of how encouragement to push back against academic stereotypes of athletes actually solidifies the existence of the stereotypes and the figurative identities that correspond to them. Similarly, the role of communication between practitioners and coaches should be critiqued because athletes' perception of academic support in a reporting relationship to the athletic domain limits the positive role an academic center plays as a hybrid space and ultimately hinders the athletes' mobility into the academic domain.

QUESTIONS FOR DISCUSSION

1. What figurative and positional identities do athletes hold on your campus? How can academic support centers work to break down stigmatized figurative identities?
2. What should be the goals for academic support centers? Are these stated goals in conflict with the goals of the university or athletic department?
3. The academic center as a hybrid space allows for an expanded notion of what constitutes competent participation. Where else do hybrid spaces exist on campuses?
4. What does learning look like in academic classrooms, athletic practice, and within the hybrid space of the academic study centers for athletes? What messages do athletes receive based on these different types of learning?

NOTES

1. I will refer to students who engage in intercollegiate athletics as "athletes" and students who do not participate in intercollegiate athletics as "students at large." This is an intentional move away from the NCAA's term of choice, "student-athlete", which is both redundant, since all people enrolled in school are students, and stigmatizing as a potential trigger for stereotype threat (Stone, Harrison & Mottley, 2012).
2. The phrase "Figured Worlds" is developed at length by anthropologists Holland, Skinner, Lachicotte and Cain (1998).
3. The concept of the "imagined community" comes from Benedict Anderson (1983). While Anderson used it to explain the rise of modern nationalism, the concept explains the sense of unity felt by members of a group despite the lack of even indirect interaction. While academics and athletics function as Figured Worlds, I argue that they are embedded within the imagined community of the larger university.
4. Interviewed staff members are referred to as Lina or Angela when addressing their interview responses, but they are simply identified as Bridge staff or instructors elsewhere.

REFERENCES

Adler, P., & Adler, P. A. (1985). From idealism to pragmatic detachment: The academic performance of college athletes. *Sociology of Education,* 58, 241–250.

Adler, P., & Adler, P.A. (1991). *Backboards and blackboards.* New York, NY: Columbia University Press.

Alesia, M. (2008, September 7). "'Special' treatment for athletes." *Indystar.com.* Retrieved from http://www.newhaven.edu/24185.pdf

Anderson, B. (1983). *Imagined communities: Reflections on the origin and spread of nationalism.* London, England: Verso.

Benson, K. F. (2000). Constructing academic inadequacy: African-American athletes' stories of schooling. *Journal of Higher Education, 71,* 223–246.

Bloor, M. (1997). Techniques of validation in qualitative research: A critical commentary. In. G. Miller & R. Dingwall (Eds.). *Context and method in qualitative research* (pp. 37–50). London, England: Sage.

Bowen, W. G., & Levin, S. A. (2003). *Reclaiming the game: College sports and educational values.* Princeton, NJ: Princeton University Press.

Charmaz, K. (1995) The logic of grounded theory. In S. Harre & V. Van Langenhove (Eds). *Rethinking methods in psychology* (pp. 27–49). London, England: Sage.

Clotfelter, C. T. (2011). *Big-time sports in American universities.* New York, NY: Cambridge University Press.

Edwards, H. (1984). The Black "dumb jock": An American sports tragedy. *College Board Review, 131,* 8–13.

Geertz, C. (1973). *The interpretation of cultures: Selected essays.* New York, NY: Basic Books.

Greeno, J. G. (2006). Learning in activity. In K. Sawyer (Ed.) *The Cambridge handbook of the learning sciences* (pp. 79-96). Cambridge, England: Cambridge University Press.

Gutiérrez, K. D., Baquedano-López, P., & Tejeda, C. (1999). Rethinking diversity: Hybridity and hybrid language practices in the third space. *Mind, Culture, and Activity, 6*(4), 286–303.

Holland, D. (2010). Symbolic worlds in time/spaces of practice: Identities and transformations. In B. Wagoner (Ed.) *Symbolic transformations: The mind in movement through culture and society* (pp. 269–283). London, England: Routledge.

Holland, D., Lachicotte, W., Skinner, D., & Cain, C. (1998). Identity *and agency in cultural worlds.* Cambridge, MA: Harvard University Press.

Hyatt, Rhonda. (2003). Barriers to persistence among African-American intercollegiate athletes: A literature review of non-cognitive variables. *College Student Journal 37,* 260–75.

Jaschik, S. (2008, September 8). "Quick takes: 'Special admits' for football, college GOP official's Obama post, William." *Inside Higher Ed.* Retrieved from http://www.insidehighered.com/news/2008/09/08/qt#ixzz2QCmM107f

Maloney, M. T., & McCormick, R. E. (1993). An examination of the role that intercollegiate athletic participation plays in academic achievement: Athletes' feats in the classroom. *Journal of Human Resources, 28,* 555–570.

Nolen, S. B., Ward, C. J., Horn, I. S., Childers, S., Campbell, S., & Mahna, K. (2008). Motivation in preservice teachers: The development of utility filters. In M. Wosnitza, S. A. Karabenick, A. Efklides & P. Nenniger (Eds.). *Contemporary motivation research: From global to local perspectives.* Ashland, OH: Hogrefe & Huber.

"North Carolina's widening academic scandal could be test case for the NCAA's newfound power." (2012, August 17). *Yahoo! Sports.* Retrieved from http://sports.yahoo.com/news/ncaaf—fbc-ncaa-north-carolina-academic-fraud-investigation.html.

Shulman, J. L., & Bowen, W. G. (2001). *The game of life: College sports and educational values.* Princeton, NJ: Princeton University Press.

Simons, H. D., Bosworth, C., Fujita, S., & Jensen, M. (2007). The athlete stigma in higher education. *College Student Journal, 41,* 251–273.

Small, M. L. (2009). How many cases do I need? On science and the logic of case selection in field-based research. *Ethnography, 10*(1), 5–38.

Stone, J., Harrison, C. K., & Mottley, J. V. (2012). Don't call me student athlete: The effect of identity priming on stereotype threat for academically engaged African-American college athletes. *Basic & Applied Social Psychology, 34,* 99–106.

Umbach, P., Palmer, M., Kuh, G., & Hannah, S. (2006) Intercollegiate athletes and effective educational practices: Winning combination or losing effort? *Research in Higher Education, 47,* 709–733.

CHAPTER 9

LOCATION, LOCATION, LOCATION

Placing Athletic Academic Support Offices

Laura M. Bernhard and Lydia F. Bell

ABSTRACT

Since the NCAA mandated academic support services for athletes in 1991, academic services have expanded immensely. Many campuses have constructed facilities on a grand scale, where size, aesthetics, and amenities are headlined while the center's location within the campus design, and how that might play a role in the academic experience of the athlete, often seems an afterthought. In response, and as a call for more data-driven practices, this chapter examines the location of academic support centers at Division 1 football bowl subdivision (FBS) institutions, seeking to better understand how the location impacts the athlete experience. To accomplish this, the physical locations of athletic facilities and athlete academic support service centers at all 125 Division 1 FBS institutions were identified in relation to each campus' academic core. Semistructured interviews were conducted with athletic academic support staff at institutions that had chosen to locate these centers close to the ac-

Making the Connection, pages 125–141

ademic heart of campus. Using administrators' voices, the benefits and challenges of locating these services at a campus' academic core were discussed as well as the implications for athletic practitioners were offered, which may have added relevance for schools considering relocation or the development of new facilities.

INTRODUCTION

In 1991, the National Collegiate Athletic Association (NCAA) established Division 1 bylaw 16.3.1.1, which stated that:

> Member institutions shall make general academic counseling and tutoring services available to all student athletes. Such counseling and tutoring services may be provided by the department of athletics or the institution's non-athletics student support services. (NCAA, 2010, p. 223)

This bylaw served to mandate and formalize the provision of academic support services throughout the NCAA Division 1 membership, and made athletic academic centers a standard part of the campus landscape (Jolly, 2008). Although Division 1 member institutions must provide such services, campuses have met the requirements in different way: facilities vary widely in terms of size, resources, mission, and offerings (Jolly). Yet, an often overlooked aspect of variation is the location of these centers, which has implications for shaping the athlete experience.

Across Division 1 (FBS)[1] campuses, most academic centers where athletes receive the mandated advising and tutoring are within, or in close proximity to, a school's athletic facilities. This placement can limit athletes' interactions with faculty, and with other students outside of the athletic department's purview, to only the credit hours spent in class each week. Given the relationship between campus engagement and various student outcomes, including retention and persistence (Astin, 1993), we must ask the question: Might locating academic support facilities in the academic core of the campus (rather than within the athletic complex, which is often on the campus' periphery) benefit the academic experience of athletes?

This chapter examines the location of academic support centers at Division 1 FBS institutions, and seeks to better understand how the location impacts the athlete experience. It begins with a review of the research on the athlete experience and explores the meaning of space and place. The methodology section outlines how we analyzed campus maps and identified potential participants as well as our process of conducting semi-structured interviews. Participants' insights are then shared and interpreted in the findings, where we discuss the benefits and challenges of locating these services at a campus' academic core, in relation to the athletes' academic experience. The chapter concludes with implications for athletic practitioners, which may have added relevance for schools considering the development of new facilities.

BACKGROUND

As a result of NCAA bylaw 16.3.1.1, and the increasing demands placed on athletes, the field of athletic academic support has grown significantly. Additionally, many high-profile athletes enter college academically underprepared, and are thrust into the spotlight and subject to criticism by the media, the community, and their peers (Broughton & Neyer, 2001), all while juggling numerous academic and athletic commitments. In response, athletic departments have expanded their personnel to include tutors, mentors, learning specialists, and team-specific advisers to help athletes adjust to the rigor of college academics within the competitive Division 1 environment. To house this growing staff, and as a recruiting tool, many institutions have remodeled or built new, grand academic facilities, bestowing the athletic academic center with a newfound level of importance (Wolverton, 2008).

Time Constraints

Intercollegiate athletes have college experiences that are distinctly different, both academically and socially, from their non-athlete peers (Astin, 1993; Watt & Moore, 2001). This difference is due in large part to the time commitments required to remain competitive at the Divison 1 level (Ferrante, Etzel, & Lantz, 1996; NCAA, 2011a). In fact, the NCAA reports that Division 1 athletes spend an average of 32 hr on athletics and 31.7 hr on academic activities per week while in season, (NCAA, 2011b), with some sports experiencing significantly more time demands. These athletes must find a way to balance the time demands of practice, competition, strength training, meetings, film reviews, and rehabilitation sessions, in addition to the academic commitments of attending class, studying, completing assignments, and taking exams. As a result, Division 1 athletes who become intensely involved in their sport, tend to be isolated from many of the effects of their peer group, which normally accompanies college attendance (Adler & Adler, 1991; Astin, 1984).

Isolation and Identity

Interaction with non-athlete peers has been shown to be particularly salient in athlete learning outcomes (Gayles & Hu, 2009). However, given athletes' time commitments, they are often sequestered in athlete-only environments close to practice facilities. This physical segregation from non-athlete peers has caused athlete subcultures to form within their given institution, which can result in social isolation (Umbach, Palmer, Kuh, & Hannah, 2006). Tinto's (1993) research highlights that such isolation, which results when "persons find themselves largely isolated from the daily life of the institution" (p. 50), can be a primary barrier to integration into the campus environment and can ultimately affect persistence (see also Comeaux & Harrison, 2011).

Another important consideration is the potential for conflict between the student and athlete identities; a duality that has been written about extensively (e.g., Adler & Adler, 1991; Yopyk & Prentice, 2005). While college students are assumed to have high academic ability and motivation, athletes are often assumed to be lacking in these very same qualities (Engstrom, Sedlacek, & McEwen, 1995; Simons, Bosworth, Fujita, & Jensen, 2007). In fact, the student identity, which is associated with a positive academic stereotype, may facilitate academic performance; while the athlete identity, with its negative connotation, may hinder students' true academic potential (Stone, 2012; Yopyk & Prentice, 2005; see also Steele & Aronson, 1995, for work on stereotype threat). Thus, for these individuals there may be an engulfment in the athlete role, if their identity (academic or athletic) is made salient, has consequences for academic performance, or if the high demands on athletes' time results in isolation from non-athlete peer groups (Adler & Adler, 1991).

Importance of Space and Place

The effect of physical location on one's identity and experience has made issues of space, place, and location pressing concerns for scholars (Jack, 2009). Space (one's physical environment) can both play a role in shaping one's identity and have implications for where one fits in the social milieu. Therefore, we see space and place as having both psychological and sociological functions.

Place identity is a term used to describe a "cognitive structure…characterized by a host of attitudes, values, thoughts, beliefs, meanings and behavior tendencies…related to the past, present, and anticipated physical settings that define and circumscribe the day-to-day existence of the person" (Proshansky, Fabian, & Kaminoff, 1983, p. 62). Thus, the spaces in which one spends his or her day can shape individual beliefs and actions, and such spaces become entwined with one's identity. At the same time, Harvey (1990) reminds us that,

> The assignment of place within a social-spatial structure indicates distinctive roles, capacities for action, and access to power within that social order...all of us, at some level of meaning, know what our place is...and to challenge what that place may be, physically as well as socially, is to challenge something fundamental in the social order. (p. 419)

Thus, while place may shape one's identity, it is frequently assigned, and decisions over *where* someone is placed (consciously or implicitly) may be indicative of social order.

As athletes balance dual roles, the location of the athletic academic support center has implications for their campus experience. Locating the center within the athletic complex—a space that emphasizes the athletic role—may create challenges in terms of academic focus and possibly activate stereotype threat.[2] Such a center may also send a message to these athletes about how they fit in as part of the campus social structure and serve to distance them from the general student body, not only physically, but also psychologically. Since it is common practice for athletic academic support services to be housed within the athletic facilities, and for such athletic facilities to be located on the periphery of the central campus (away from academic and student affairs departments) (Jordan & Denson, 1990), we must consider whether this best serves athletes. Indeed, many campuses require athletes to traverse long distances (in some cases through nature preserves or woods, and across train tracks or rivers), to reach athletic facilities (see Figures 9.1 and 9.2). However, there are examples of Division 1 FBS campuses that have chosen to locate their athletic academic support centers within the academic core of campus. This chapter examines how those spaces impact the athlete experience at these unique institutions.

METHODS

Campus maps were downloaded from each Division 1 FBS institution's official website and saved as PDFs. Using each institution's website, map keys, and/or interactive campus map web-based tools, the academic and athletic cores and locations of the athletic academic support centers were identified. The building housing the academic support facility and the perimeters of each core were drawn on individual maps for visual analysis using Adobe Acrobat (see Figures 9.1–9.3).

The academic core of a campus was determined by identifying that campus' main library and the buildings that typically house undergraduate general

Figure 9.1 Map of University of Missouri. *Source:* Map courtes of the University Relations at University of Missouri.

education curricula (e.g., psychology, social sciences, English, humanities). The athletic core was identified as the area surrounding the athletic administrative offices—specifically that housing the athletic director—and the majority of the competition facilities (e.g., natatorium, football stadium, track). The location of the athletic academic support offices was determined by visiting each campus' athletic department website and looking for documentation that gave the name of the building in which the center was housed. We were able to locate such a building at each institution. Of 125 coded maps, we identified 16 (13%) with athlete academic support programs located in or adjacent to the academic core of campus (for example, see Figure 9.3). All of the maps were extracted from campus websites between August 2012 and

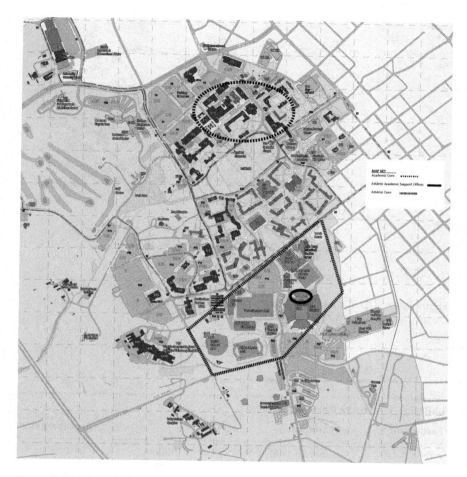

Figure 9.2 Map of Virginia Polytechnic Institute and State University. *Source:* Map courtesy of the Virginia Tech Marketing & Publications.

May 2013, and the coding of these maps reflects the physical layout of these campuses during the 2012–2013 academic year.

As we were particularly interested in learning more about the athletic academic support centers located within or on the periphery of the academic core of campus, a series of questions was designed to be answered by a departmental representative at each of these campuses. A request to participate was sent via email to the athletic academic director—and in some cases also the assistant or associate director—at each of these campuses. In total, four campuses participated in the phone interview process, and three responded via email; all participating institutions are listed in Table 9.1.

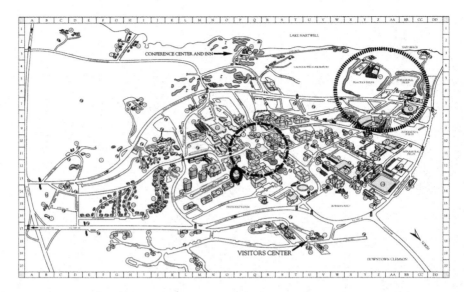

Figure 9.3 Map of Clemson University. *Source:* Map courtesy of the director of creative services, Clemson University.

TABLE 9.1 Study Participants

Participant	Institution	Title	Reporting Line
Robert Baker	University of Memphis	Director, Athletic Academic Services	Vice Provost
Rebecca Bowman	Clemson University	Associate AD for Academic Services[1]	Provost
Jessica Clarke Leger	University of Louisiana, Lafayette	Associate AD for Academics and Compliance/SWA	Provost and AD
Tommy Powell	Iowa State University	Associate AD for Academic Services	AD
Pamela Riegle	Ball State University	Director, Student-Athlete Support Services	Assoc. Provost
Jill Shields	Kansas State University	Senior Associate AD/ SWA, Director of Student Services	AD
Derek Van Rheenen	University of California, Berkeley	Director, Athletic Study Center	Vice Provost

[1] Retired in 2013

FINDINGS

Semistructured interviews with athletic academic support administrators at campuses where the athletic academic center was located within or near the academic core of campus, were conducted to explore their perceptions of how the physical location of these centers impacted the athlete experience. The main themes that emerged from the interview data include: convenience of location and how a center's location allowed for an academic focus, created a safe space, facilitated interaction with other students, and integrated campus services; and the challenges placed on administrators in preserving the location of these centers due to the athletic "arms race."

Convenience of Location

The most obvious benefit of being near the academic core of campus was the convenience of location: a factor noted by all of our participants. Pamela Riegle, the director of student-athlete support services at Ball State University, explained, "Like most campuses, our athlete facilities are on the end of campus, so we are much more accessible during the day in our present location [in the main quad]. Students can pop in." This finding also acknowledges athletes' hectic schedules and the benefit of being able to maximize their time during the academic block of their day. As Jessica Clarke Leger, associate athletic director for academics and compliance at the University of Louisiana at Lafayette, explained, "An on-campus location supports our initiative of prioritizing daytime study hall. We encourage our student athletes to complete homework assignments between classes." Jill Shields, a senior associate athletic director at Kansas State University, furthered this connection, underscoring how the location benefits academic learning, mainly by allowing students to complete work during the day when they are best able to focus.

> Having a facility on campus has been vital to the success of our program. Because our main [athletic] facility is two miles from the heart of campus... the [academic] facility is more convenient. [It] benefits the student athletes academically as many of them can now complete their commitments to us before supper, whereas before, they had to come back in the evening... when they were exhausted.

Thus, participants felt that having a centrally-located academic center improved the academic experience of athletes by allowing them to maximize their time in the campus academic core and complete assignments during the day when they were presumably more alert. Limiting travel time between classroom space and the academic support center may also reduce some of the stress related to time demands previously identified by the NCAA (2011b), amongst others.

Academic Focus

Participants believed the physical separation of the academic center from the athletics facilities served to allow the space to have a purely academic focus. Indeed, this demarcation of athletic and academic spaces can be a visual cue for the role athletes are expected to play when they are in the center, signaling a clear delineation between their dual identities. As Tommy Powell, an associate athletic director at Iowa State University said, this separation is "valuable for our student athletes . . . to come and feel like they're in an academic building. I think our coaches like the fact that it's here and . . . I like the fact that we don't have any distractions when they get here." The location of the center within the academic core of campus, also extended and maintained the academic focus, thereby helping the staff make the best use of athletes' limited time. As Rebecca Bowman, associate athletic director of academic services at Clemson University explained:

> We are able to sustain the academic interest for the academic block of the day. We try to have our students schedule their tutoring between classes and schedule their study time between classes. Particularly [for] our students who are academically at-risk because of their preparation, we have them meeting with learning specialists during the day. So I think that we do sustain an academic focus for a longer period of time compared to if we were not located near the classroom buildings.

Here, our participants drew connections between physical space and rhetorical practice or pedagogy (Jack, 2009). They elicited the benefits of having the academic center separate from the athletics facilities and near the academic core of campus as it demarcated the space as an academic one, thereby activating the student identity and leading to a more productive use of time (Yopyk & Prentice, 2005).

Safe Space

While having athletic facilities removed from the main campus may protect high-profile athletes from the general campus population (Broughton & Neyer, 2001), our participants perceived being located away from athletics as providing security for their athletes in a different way: limiting interactions with coaches during a time of academic focus. Even though Derek Van Rheenen, the director of the athletic study center at University of California at Berkeley, acknowledged advantages to being located near athletics: so "a coach can just walk down the hall and talk to an academic adviser and that they're on the same page." He went on to say:

But that has its own negatives, too, in the sense that neither the student ath-letes oftentimes, nor my advisers or tutors, want to have a coach hovering over them...we have had football players, for example, who are very clear that they want to be away from the stadium for their academics because they don't want that feeling where the coach is constantly on them.

Bob Baker, the director of athletic academic services at the University of Memphis, echoed this sentiment saying, "I don't want a coach coming by study hall every day. I want them to leave us alone and let us do our jobs. I mean, I don't go by practice and try and tell them how to coach better."

This distancing from coaches is also a very real compliance concern as the NCAA has strict rules governing the provision of academic support. To ensure academic honesty and compliance with NCAA bylaws, Bowman (Clemson) explained, "We don't allow our students to do anything over [there] with coaches...we are trying to do everything that we can to pre-vent the appearance of academic impropriety." In this way, the physical separation of academics from athletics helps to clearly delineate the role of coaches in the athlete experience, and may allow the students an op-portunity to balance these competing identities that have been a focus of the literature.

Student Interaction

Van Rheenen (UC) noted that traditional athletics facilities "very much segregate the student-athlete population—both geographically and social-ly," which can be "problematic." Participants spoke of the increased possi-bilities for student interaction and integration resulting from locating their centers within or adjacent to the academic core. Discussing UC's academic center, Van Rheenen continued, "I think it benefits them because they are more fully integrated in the campus life...they see other students who may look like them but are not student athletes." Such encounters may encour-age athletes and non athletes alike to extend their social circles and engage with one another while also reinforcing the normality of academic behavior for athletes. As an example, Ball State athletes share tutoring spaces with non athletes helping to create the sense of a unified student body and lead-ing their director, Riegle, to assert, "I don't think [our student athletes] feel isolated from the general population of campus in any way." Powell (Iowa) furthered this idea, identifying the increased interaction as a way to break down barriers between athletes and their non-athlete peers and disprove stereotypes. He said, "I think it's great for anytime you have athletes who actually...who the normal students see interacting in their academic man-ner....I think it's good for the normal students to see our athletes coming to study and then working and interacting. I think that's a big part of this."

This opportunity for interaction between these two populations could reduce the potential for social isolation amongst the athlete population as identified by Umbach et al. (2006).

Integration With Campus

As the centers' location provides increased opportunities for interaction between athletes and their non-athlete peers, it also provides the structure to support integration—both for students and staff. Riegle (Ball State) noted how sharing space with other academic offices served to incorporate athletes into the larger system of campus support, with this integration ultimately fulfilling the academic center's mission:

> From our office's inception, the BSU philosophy has been to allow the student-athlete population to experience college as close as possible to a regular student. We therefore use the same tutors and same advising system as the regular students...and our students go the same place to study as other students on campus.

Many of our participants also spoke of the benefits of their center's location in enabling them to collaborate with other campus offices and ultimately offering students more comprehensive support. Baker (Memphis) remarked, "Because we are centrally located on campus and our staff interacts with admissions, and financial aid, and the faculty a lot...those relationships directly benefit our student athletes." At UC, the athletic study center is located in a building that also houses the office for students with disabilities, and various resource centers. This creates what Van Rheenen claims to be the most "student-centric building on campus." This model of being separate from athletics, but integrated with other campus offices, allows athletes to connect with people who may help them to explore their other identities and, as Van Rheenen believes, "is the model that is most appropriate for academic support for student athletes if you [want] to...integrate them into the general student body."

Adding another dimension, Powell (Iowa) discussed how the central location and integration with other support services encouraged a collaborative environment between units. Discussing his center, he said, "we open it up to review sessions" where professors will hold study sessions for to all students in the center's conference room. Powell viewed this as "just a great way of giving back," and such acts of reciprocity serve to further integrate his office with the larger campus, showing that sharing spaces can also build relationships.

Arms Race Tensions

In addition to the normal growing pains of serving the ever-increasing college-going population, athletic departments have long been involved in an "arms race" that continues to shape the Division 1-FBS landscape. The competition for top recruits means it is not just about having ample space for students and staff, but about how prospective students and their families perceive the look and feel of the space. As such, our participants indicated that their centers were often integrated into recruiting tours and cited the importance placed upon not only the services provided but also the physical places where they occur. For example, Iowa State completed construction on a $10 million academic center in 2007, and director Powell reflected:

> Most of our coaches lead with us, which is nice . . . because the university sells itself, but I think the . . . building just kind of helps that process. . . . You know, there's a lot of artwork in the building, so coming in you feel like you're coming into an academic environment and I think that's hugely important.

While such a modern center has become a recruiting highlight for Iowa State, Baker spoke of feeling pressure from the coaching staff to relocate Memphis' outdated center. He noted,

> We have outgrown this facility by leaps and bounds. And I think from a recruiting perspective it hurts us, because I mean this is a nice facility—it's two floors, and it's pretty big—but it's not anything like what some of the bigger schools have.

In addition to feeling pressured to modernize and grow his center to keep up with benchmark athletic programs, he also indicated pressure to relocate, "The coaches very much want an academic center that is close in proximity to where their athletes lift weights and work out so that [the coaches] can very easily walk by study hall and check on [them]." Across the country, Van Rheenen (UC), felt similar tensions:

> If you look at our center and the building we're in and all that it is . . . it pales by comparison . . . (in our conference) we're now, I think, feeling a lot of the same pressures in terms of recruiting and competing . . . as good as our services are—and that may be philosophically and structurally—that's great. I think there's also going to be some criticism of like, "Well you guys just don't do enough." . . . I think that the arms race is going to impact, you know, it already has impacted all of us.

IMPLICATIONS FOR ATHLETIC PROFESSIONALS

In this arms race, where each institution fights to distinguish itself in a highly competitive recruitment landscape, facilities have taken on increased significance. Academic support centers, in particular, have been included in these facility upgrades, with institutions across the country constructing larger and more impressive centers, as well as increasing the number of staff and services offered. Even as researchers and practitioners alike have considered how to better support athletes athletically, academically, and emotionally, the significance of *where* such services are provided seems rarely considered. As institutions consider building new facilities or renovating old ones, it is important to consider the classic real estate adage of "location, location, location"—not just for the tangible pros and cons of the location itself, but also for the impact the location may have on the athlete experience.

As campuses grow and renovate, new facilities will often be constructed on the periphery of campus where there is more open space. Yet, we encourage schools to reflect on the benefits raised by participants in this study, of having the athletic academic center near or within the academic core of campus, and to ask developers and practitioners to consider the following questions when making informed decisions:

- What does the location of this facility imply about its purpose? What messages might this send to athletes, coaches, the general student body, faculty, and recruits about the academic aspect of the athlete experience?
- What sort of relationships will be facilitated and strengthened due to the location of this facility?
- What individuals require access to this facility, and what is the frequency of such access?
- How will the location of this building play a role in the academic performance and experience of these college athletes?

In order to answer these questions, practitioners must draw on existing scholarship and gather original data from various campus stakeholders. These data can come in a variety of forms and from a variety of sources. Examples may include visual data from campus maps or office configurations, content analysis of mission statements or reporting structures, and qualitative data from focus groups with athletes, coaches, and athletic support staff. Data collection can occur both within a campus (cross-department comparisons), as well as between multiple campuses considering how peer institutions are using spaces. Perhaps this work will uncover existing models that more fully integrate athletes into the campus structure. Then this process could gather important information not only on the experiences of those who frequent the facilities, but also allow stakeholders to participate in the planning process, which will create a culture of data-driven practices and perhaps ultimately influence how athletic department facilities are designed and utilized.

QUESTIONS FOR DISCUSSION

1. Consider the location of academic support services for athletes at your institution. How might this space play a role in shaping the identities of the athletes who frequent this center?
2. What might this location signal to athletes regarding the social order of campus? What might it signal to non-athlete students? What meaning does this space convey about the history and role of sport at your institution?
3. Given the concerns over the safety and protection of college athletes, and the role location plays in providing both, what is the ideal campus location for athletes to receive academic support services?
4. College athletes may struggle with balancing the dual identities of student and athlete. Might locating academic centers within athletic facilities help to integrate or confuse these roles? Or would doing so prioritize the athletic domain?
5. While certain services or facilities may be segregated for athletes for practical purposes, what other areas or programs could campuses use to increase opportunities for interaction between athletes and non-athletes (e.g., dining halls, orientation, residence halls, first-year seminars)?
6. This chapter notes both advantages and disadvantages in locating an athletic academic support center close to an academic core of campus. What is your recommendation for the location of academic support centers?

NOTES

1. FBS is one of three subdivisions in Division 1. Member institutions field football teams that may participate in post-season bowl games. These are the schools most often cited in the media and literature—often referred to as "big-time" college sports.
2. Stereotype threat refers to an instance when someone who fears confirming a negative stereotype about a group with which he or she identifies, has a physiological response (reduced cognitive and emotional resources) that causes him or her to perform more poorly than when the stereotype was not acti-

vated (Steele & Aronson, 1995). For example, athletes are often confronted with the *dumb jock* stereotype. Thus, when the athlete identity is emphasized (e.g., by being in an athletic space), students may not perform as well on academic tasks as they would have otherwise because of the anxiety prompted by concerns over confirming that stereotype.

REFERENCES

Adler, P. A., & Adler, P. (1991). *Backboards & blackboards: College athletes and role engulfment.* New York, NY: Columbia University Press.

Astin, A. W. (1984). Student involvement: A developmental theory for higher education. *Journal of college student personnel, 25,* 297–308.

Astin, A. W. (1993). *What matters in college? Four critical years revisited.* San Francisco, CA: Jossey-Bass.

Broughton, E., & Neyer, M. (2001). Advising and counseling student athletes. *New Directions for Student Services, 93,* 47–53.

Comeaux, E. & Harrison, C. K. (2011). A conceptual model of academic success for student athletes. *Educational Researcher, 4,* 235–245.

Engstrom, C., Sedlacek, W., & McEwen, M. (1995). Faculty attitudes toward male revenue and nonrevenue student athletes. *Journal of College Student Development, 36,* 217–227.

Ferrante, A. P., Etzel, E., & Lantz, C. (1996). Counseling college student athletes: The problem,the need. In E. Fetzel, A. P. Ferrante, & J. W. Pinkney (Eds.). *Counseling college student athletes: Issues and interventions,* (2nd ed.), 1–18. Morgantown, WV: Fitness Information Technology.

Gayles, J. G., & Hu, S. (2009). The influence of student engagement and sport participation on college outcomes among Division 1 student athletes. *The Journal of Higher Education, 80,* 315–333.

Harvey, D. (1990). Between space and time: Reflections on the geographical imagination. *Annals of the Association of American Geographers, 80,* 418–434.

Jack, J. (2009). Space, place, and the public face of composition. *College English, 72*(2), 188–198.

Jolly, C. J. (2008). Raising the question #9: Is the student-athlete population unique? And why should we care? *Communication Education, 57*(1), 145–151.

Jordan, J. M., & Denson, E. L. (1990). Student services for athletes: A model for enhancing the student-athlete experience. *Journal of Counseling & Development, 69,* 95–97.

National Collegiate Athletic Association. (2010). *2010-11 NCAA Division 1 manual: Constitutional operating bylaws, administrative bylaws* [Effective August 1, 2010]. Indianapolis, IN: NCAA.

National Collegiate Athletic Association. (2011a). *Examining the student athlete experience through the NCAA GOALS and SCORE studies.* Presented at the 2011 convention of the NCAA, San Antonio, TX.

National Collegiate Athletic Association. (2011b). *Division I results from the NCAA GOALS study on the student-athlete experience.* Presented at the 2011 annual meeting and symposium of FARA (Faculty Athletics Representatives Association), San Diego, CA.

Proshansky, H. M., Fabian, A. K., & Kaminoff, R. (1983). Place-identity: Physical world socialization of the self. *Journal of Environmental Psychology 3*(1), 57–83.

Simons, H. D., Bosworth, C., Fujita, S., & Jensen, M. (2007). The athlete stigma in higher education. *College Student Journal, 41*, 251–273.

Steele, C. M., & Aronson, J. (1995). Stereotype threat and the intellectual test performance of African Americans. *Journal of Personality and Social Psychology, 69*, 797–811.

Stone, J. (2012). A hidden toxicity in the term "student-athlete": Stereotype threat for athletes in the college classroom. *Wake Forest Journal of Law & Policy, 2*, 179.

Tinto, V. (1993). *Leaving college: Rethinking the causes and cures of student attrition* (2nd ed.) Chicago, IL: University of Chicago Press.

Umbach, P. D., Palmer, M. M., Kuh, G. D., & Hannah, S. J. (2006). Intercollegiate athletics and effective educational practices: Winning combination or losing effort? *Research in Higher Education, 47*, 709–733.

Watt, S. K., & Moore, J. L. (2001). Who are student athletes? *New Directions for Student Services, 93*, 7–18.

Wolverton, B. (2008, September 5). "Rise in fancy academic centers for athletes raises questions of fairness." *The Chronicle of Higher Education*. Retrieved from http://chronicle.com.

Yopyk, D. J., & Prentice, D. A. (2005). Am I an athlete or a student? Identity salience and stereotype threat in student–athletes. Basic and Applied Social Psychology, *27*, 329–336.

CHAPTER 10

REFLECTIONS ON DATA-INFORMED PRACTICES

Elizabeth Broughton

I was invited to share my perspective and predictions for best practices within academic support centers for athletes. I am truly honored to provide my input regarding these issues for the development of evidence-based, data-driven strategies for academic support centers.

Over a decade ago, my coauthor and I provided a normative review of the current status of academic advising and counseling provided to student athletes (Broughton & Neyer, 2001). We summarized four, practice-based models as necessary for integration within athletic academic support centers: academic advising, life-skills development, clinical and mental health counseling, and performance-enhancing approaches (sports psychology). In the same article, we described a recommended academic developmental model, and provided supportive institutional examples as cutting-edge support center models.

As I reflect upon the past decade (during which I served as a faculty athletics representative at a Division 1 institution), I am not convinced that data-driven best practices for academic support centers for athletes have advanced much beyond our original normative review. Sadly, some academic support centers still remain very similar to the summary description by Shriberg and Brodzinski's (1984), which focused only on eligibility and scheduling. So even today, some academic support centers are still only providing athletes with academic tutoring and minimal advisement for class.

During this decade, while athletic academic support centers maintained status quo, the emphasis on academic reform did not. Due to low graduation rates among college athletes in specific sports, the NCAA has instituted reform through the implementation of the academic performance rate (APR), which was developed to improve graduation rates. As a result, the academic support center's main function has been to retain and help athletes graduate. With the new academic APR standard, many academic support centers have hired more staff members to monitor athlete academic success, thus limiting their work to managing eligibility and meeting APR standards. But they did not invest in the athletes' psychological well-being. For instance, there is little emphasis on the importance of the athletes' psychological well-being, cognitive learning, personal development, and career exploration, in the National Association of Academic Advisors for Athletics' (N4A) (the leading professional association for athletic advising), guidelines and proficiency standards for athletic advising support centers (N4A, 2015). Currently, there are only 30 NCAA institutions listed as meeting the N4A advising certification program. On a related note in the academic arena, the academic program review is an essential practice for all academic disciplines. Furthermore, institutions are regularly measured according to the standards for regional and national accreditation. But, the only significant change among support centers in the last 10 years, may have been the N4A proficiency standards and the hiring of more staff to maintain athlete eligibility, boost retention, and insure graduation rates.

A promising model through which to improve retention and graduation rates that may support athletic advising centers, is the recent Comeaux and Harrison (2011) conceptual approach. This conceptual model provides structure for academic success centers, athletic departments, and researchers. Their conceptual framework examines evidence-based research conducted on college student learning, such as the seminal work of Tinto (1987) and Bean and Metzner (1985) on attrition and commitment, and provides a structure for recruiting and retaining athletes. Comeaux and Harrison's model describes the various factors that may impact academic success for student athletes, such as, commitment, social systems, and social and academic integration. This model can provide academic support centers with a guide for working with college athletes.

In addition to the Comeaux and Harrison model, this decade saw an increase in college athlete research. Although the research is not directly related to academic athletic support centers, the research provides significant information to assist with academic support center staff. Several studies have explored different athlete functions, such as, demonstrating a positive athlete experience (Potuto & O"Hanlon, 2007), describing the athlete socialization process (Marx, Huffmon, & Doyle, 2008), exploring academic and athletic motivations (Gaston-Gayles, 2004), and fostering athlete career construction (Navarro, inpress). Additionally, college athlete research presentations have increased at numerous academic and student affairs conferences, including the American Educational Research Association (AERA), the Association for the Study of Higher Education (ASHE), the National Association of Student Personnel Administrators (NASPA), and the American College Personnel Association (ACPA). Even the NCAA briefly supported a research agenda. Other notable endeavors were that several institutions recognized the potential training and research required in athletics. Several institutions are providing specific academic studies in coursework and research on athletics and athletes, such as Oklahoma University's doctoral program in adult and higher education with a core emphasis on intercollegiate athletic administration, and the center for leadership in athletics at the University of Washington. All of these increases in research are significant in that they may impact the success of, or provide improvements for, athlete academic support centers.

Overall, the changes seen during this decade have advanced the research on athletes. However, more research is needed to improve evidence-based data for academic support centers. In an effort to improve athletic academic support centers, researchers and practitioners might consider the following issues and questions related to academic oversight.

ACADEMIC OVERSIGHT

Currently, the NCAA rules require the appointment of a faculty athletic representative (FAR) for all NCAA institutions. This faculty member acts as a buffer between athletics and academics to bridge institutional control, academic integrity, and athlete well-being. There are various best practices set for the FAR; however, little evidence-based research is known regarding the FARs impact on academics and athletes. Questions remain regarding the evidence that this FAR model is a best practice for athletics (and the college athlete) and academic support centers. Beyond the FAR, should institutions require more oversight? If so, what evidenced-based data exists for this need? And what is an evidenced-based practice for FARs' current role in academic support centers?

Furthermore, what is the best organizational practice model for athletic academic support centers to follow? Should the support center be organized administratively within the academic core, or within the athletic core? Do we know whether one organizational core demonstrates a better practice than the other? Is there evidence-based data to bridge the academic and athletic cores? Instead of calling for academic reforms (Knight Commission, 1991, 2001, & 2010), what best practices exist between the academic and athletic cores for athletic academic support centers?

Other academic oversight concerns are the influence and impact of coaches and athletic personnel, with regards to academic support centers. Since coaches and other personnel spend enormous time with athletes, what evidence-based data exists for athletic personnel's support or impact on academic support centers? Sharp and Sheilley (2008) noted several institutional responsibilities and addressed the role of coaches, faculty, and academic and athletic administrators, and outlined strategies to be developed to improve the athletes' well-being. Yet, little research has been conducted in this regard.

And finally, this book was developed to share and explore evidence-based data or best practices within athletic academic support centers. My question is whether we have evidence-based data to answer the following questions:

- What are the differences among the NCAA divisions regarding academic athletic support centers?
- What do we know about the academic preparation and training of academic athletic support center staff members? For instance, among those advising athletes, is having an athletic background more useful in advising, than doing so without a background? What proficiencies should academic support center staff be developing through professional training?
- What evidenced-based advising model is used in academic athletic advising centers (i.e., motivational, developmental, appreciative advising, counseling)?
- What best-practice model exists to identify cognitive impairment or other cognitive disability among athletes in academic support centers?
- What are the best practices for career exploration and development for support centers?
- Lastly, how much do we understand about the athlete culture and academic athletic support centers?

SUMMARY

The assertion that college athletics is in a crisis is a major understatement. Incidences involving academic integrity are still a major issue. Support centers are integral to the academic success of athletes. Thus, it is imperative that we consider the impact of support centers on athletes, and that we also continue to develop evidence-based data to remain true to academics and the athletes' academic and personal development, as well as athletic success.

My purpose within this article has been to reflect on events and developments during the past decade and to address future issues. However, I may have raised more questions than provided answers. I encourage practitioners and the researchers who contributed to this book to continue to explore evidenced-based practices for athletes and academic support centers for athletes.

REFERENCES

Bean, J. P., & Metzner, B. S. (1985). A conceptual model of nontraditional undergraduate student attrition. *Review of Educational Research, 55*, 485–540.

Broughton, E., & Neyer, M. (2001). Advising and counseling student athletes. *New Directions for Student Services, 93*, 47–53.

Comeaux, E., & Harrison, C. K. (2011). A conceptual model for academic success for student athletes. *Educational Researcher, 40*, 235–245.

Gaston-Gayles, J. L. (2004). Examining academic and athletic motivation among student athletes at a Division 1 university. *Journal of College Student Development, 45*, 75–83.

Knight Foundation Commission on Intercollegiate Athletics. (1991). *Reports of the Knight Foundation commission of intercollegiate athletics.* Charlotte, NC.: Knight Foundation.

Knight Foundation Commission on Intercollegiate Athletics. (2001). *A call to action: Reconnecting college sports and higher education.* Charlotte, NC.: Knight Foundation.

Knight Foundation Commission on Intercollegiate Athletics. (2010). *Restoring the balance: Dollars, values, and the future of college sports.* Charlotte, NC.: Knight Foundation, 2010.

Marx, J., Huffmon, S., & Doyle, A. (2008). "The student-athlete model and the socialization of intercollegiate athletes." *Athletic Insight, 10*(1). Retrieved from http://www.athleticinsight.com/Vol10Iss1/StudentAthleteModel.htm

National Association of Academic Advisors for Athletics' (N4A) (2015). Retrieved from http://www.nacda.com/nfoura/programcertinstitutions.html

Navarro, K. (In press). Preparation for life after sport: Data-informed practices for 21st century student-athlete career development programs. In E. Comeaux (Ed.) *Making the connection: Data-informed practices in academic support centers for college athletes* (pp. 10–21). Charlotte, NC: Information Age.

Potuto, J. R., & O'Hanlon, J. (2007). National study of student athletes regarding their experiences as college students. *College Student Journal, 41*, 947–966.

Sharp, L. A., & Sheilley, H. K. (2008). The institution's obligations to athletes. *New Directions for Higher Education, 142*, 103–113.

Shriberg, A., & Brodzinski, F. R. (Eds.) (1984). Rethinking services for college athletes. *New Directions for Student Services, 26*, San Francisco, CA: Jossey-Bass.

Tinto, V. (1987). *Leaving college: Rethinking the causes and cures of student departure.* Chicago, IL: University of Chicago Press.

ABOUT THE EDITOR

Eddie Comeaux is an associate professor of higher education in the graduate school of education at the University of California, Riverside. Dr. Comeaux's research interests include college student engagement, intercollegiate athletics, and diversity competence and leadership in student affairs. He has authored numerous peer-reviewed articles in major journals including *Educational Researcher, Journal of Intercollegiate Sport, Journal of College Student Development,* and *Sociology of Sport Journal.* Comeaux is the cofounder and former chair of the Research Focus on Education and Sport Special Interest Group of the American Educational Research Association, and he is the editor of a new textbook, *Introduction to Intercollegiate Athletics* (Johns Hopkins University Press). He has also developed the Career Transition Scorecard, an action-oriented approach designed to help bridge the gap between research and practice in academic support centers for athletes. Prior to earning his doctorate at the University of California, Los Angeles, Comeaux was drafted out of University of California, Berkeley, in the amateur free draft by the Texas Rangers baseball organization, and spent four years playing professionally.

ABOUT THE CONTRIBUTORS

Lydia F. Bell is an associate director of research for academic performance at the National Collegiate Athletic Association. Formerly, Dr. Bell was an assistant professor of practice and director of Project SOAR in the Center for the Study of Higher Education at the University of Arizona. She has also worked in student affairs as an academic advisor at Pima Community College in Tucson, Arizona, and as the coordinator of student community service programs at Bowdoin College in Brunswick, Maine. Bell received her doctorate in language, reading and culture and a master's in higher education from the University of Arizona, and her bachelor's in government, legal studies and sociology from Bowdoin College. She served as the chair of the American Educational Research Association SIG Research Focus on Education and Sport from 2010–2013, and is on the editorial board for the *Journal for the Study of Sports and Athletes in Education.*

Laura M. Bernhard is a doctoral candidate in the higher education program at the graduate school of education and information studies at the University of California, Los Angeles. Her research interests include the college experiences and transition of both student-athletes and students of color, and her dissertation examines diversity in athletic departments at the staff level. Since completing her undergraduate degree, Laura has worked in student-athlete development and academic support at the University of California, Berkeley, the University of North Carolina, and the University of California, Los Angeles. In addition to her work in athletics, Bernhard is also highly active in the girls' lacrosse community, coaching at both the

Making the Connection, pages 151–155
Copyright © 2015 by Information Age Publishing
All rights of reproduction in any form reserved.

college and high school elite club level, as well as working numerous camps and clinics.

Elizabeth Broughton is a professor of educational leadership in the college of education at Eastern Michigan University and serves as the coordinator of the higher education program. Her research interests involve student-athletes, student affairs, and career development. Prior to her faculty position, Broughton was a student affairs practitioner at the University of Florida. Her background in intercollegiate athletics is diverse: She participated in two collegiate varsity sports, played professional tennis, and was a head tennis coach at a Division I institution. Recently she completed seven years as a faculty athletics representative at Eastern Michigan University.

Anne Browning is the director of academic support programs in undergraduate academic affairs and a lecturer in the college of education at the University of Washington. Browning's research focuses on the intersection of athletics and academics in higher education, specifically looking at academic pathways for intercollegiate athletes. Browning works to connect and integrate academic support for athletes with broader campus initiatives. Her current work looks at building resilience curriculum for athletes and students at large. Browning was a two-sport athlete at Harvard University, playing soccer in the fall and rowing in the winter and spring. She trained with the United States Rowing National Team for several years before hanging up her oars and pursuing a career in higher education.

Joseph N. Cooper is an assistant professor in the Neag School of Education at the University of Connecticut. Cooper's research interests focus on the intersection of race, sport, culture, and education. His current research focuses on identifying the key influences that facilitate positive educational and holistic development outcomes for Black students who participate in intercollegiate athletics. He has published in peer-reviewed journals such as *Race, Ethnicity and Education, Journal of Sport and Social Issues*, and *Journal of Intercollegiate Sport*. Prior to his current position, Cooper earned his bachelor's degrees in recreation administration and sociology as well as his master's degree in sport administration from the University of North Carolina at Chapel Hill. He earned his doctoral degree in kinesiology with a concentration in sport management and policy from the University of Georgia.

Rebecca E. Crandall is a doctoral student in educational research and policy analysis, with a specialization in higher education administration at North Carolina State University. Her research focuses on religion and spirituality in higher education, with particular attention directed toward the spirituality of student athletes. She also explores topics related to student-athlete success and campus religious and worldview diversity. Crandall's professional background includes service as the director of student involvement at Houston Baptist University and time spent as a Baptist campus minister/chaplain at the University of Louisiana at Monroe and the University of Miami. Currently, she works as a graduate research assistant for the office of assessment in the division of academic and student affairs at North Carolina State University and as a research associate for a project: Cooperation in a pluralistic world: A national study of college students' engagement with religious diversity.

Joy Gaston Gayles is an associate professor of higher education in the department of leadership, policy and adult and higher education at North Carolina State University. Gayles' research focuses on college student access and success, particularly for student athletes, women, and underrepresented minorities in STEM fields. Equity and diversity are themes that cut across all areas of her research agenda. Her research has been published in outlets such as the *Journal of Higher Education, Research in Higher Education, Journal of College Student Development,* and *Innovative Higher Education* to name a few. Gayles is a former student athlete and received a post-graduate scholarship from the NCAA to support her graduate studies. She also worked as an academic advisor and coordinator of student athlete advising at The Ohio State University. Gayles recently received the 2014 Diamond Honoree Award from American College Personnel Association (ACPA) for her contributions to the field of higher education and student affairs.

Whitney N. Griffin is a graduate of the educational psychology learning sciences program at the University of Washington. She is currently a postdoctoral fellow at the University of California, Riverside. Her research draws on several different domains such as neuropsychology, mild traumatic brain injury, revenue generating college sports, and race. Griffin's dissertation investigates how Black football players with concussions and/or learning disabilities cope with negative stereotypes of athletic and academic performance. Through her fellowship, she builds on Claude Steele's concept of stereotype threat to develop effective strategies that diffuse negative stigmas of Black football players. *Cognition, Intelligence, and Achievement* and *Annals of Dyslexia* are some peer-reviewed journals in which her research is published. She has also written a chapter in the forthcoming book, *Scandals in College Sports.*

C. Keith Harrison has over two decades of university research, teaching and service experience at the community college level (Cerritos College, Fullerton College, and Cypress College in California) and university level (Washington State University, Indiana University, University of Michigan, Arizona State University, and the University of Central Florida). His career and research focus is in a few areas: the student-athlete and professional athlete experience; diversity and inclusion issues related to gender and race relations in education, business, sport and entertainment; and the marketing of emerging multicultural demographics in the global environment in education, sport and entertainment. Currently Harrison is a consultant and researcher for the National Football League, where he advises the league on a wide variety of matters related to occupational mobility, consumer marketing with a focus on the female demographic, and other areas.

Mary F. Howard-Hamilton is the Raleigh Holmstedt distinguished professor at Indiana State University. Her research expertise is in the area of multiculturalism and diversity, publishing such books as: *Diverse Millennial Students in College, Multiculturalism on Campus—Theories, Models, and Practices for Understanding Diversity and Creating Inclusion; Unleashing Suppressed Voices on College Campuses–Diversity Issues in Higher Education;* and *Standing on the Outside Looking In–Underrepresented Students' Experiences in Advanced Degree Programs.* Howard-Hamilton has published several articles related to student athletes, most notably: "African-American Female Athletes—Issues, Implications, and Imperatives for Educators" in the ASHE reader series *Sports and Athletics in Higher Education;* "Theoretical Foundations" in *The Handbook of College Athletics and Recreation Administration;* "Student Development Theory" in *Advising Student-Athletes—A Collaborative Approach to Success;* and "New Directions for Student Services" in *Student Services for Athletes.* Howard-Hamilton is a member of the editorial board for *Journal for the Study of Sports and Athletes in Education.*

Kristina Navarro is an assistant professor of education and coordinator of the higher-education leadership program at the University of Wisconsin in Whitewater. She holds a joint appointment as a lecturer in the department of counseling psychology at the University of Wisconsin in Madison. As a scholar and practitioner, Navarro served as an athletics administrator for six years working with the University of North Carolina at Chapel Hill's Carolina Leadership Academy and at the University of Wisconsin at Madison's Badger Life Skills Academy prior to becoming a faculty member. She continues to serve as a faculty liaison for student-athlete development programs at the University of Wisconsin at Madison and the University of Wisconsin at Whitewater. She currently serves on an NCAA action team charged with developing a national student-athlete development curriculum and has published numerous articles and book chapters focused on the student-athlete experience. Navarro is a former student athlete at the Division 1 and 3 levels where she competed in the sports of rowing and track and field.

Janet Rasmussen is the athletic director at Edgewater High School in Orlando, Florida. She has spent the last four years working in interscholastic athletics, helping her coaches develop ways to motivate student athletes on the field and in the classroom. While completing her doctoral degree in curriculum and instruction at the University of Central Florida, Rasmussen was an adjunct with the DeVos Sport Business Management Program. Rasmussen's research interests include academic and athletic motivation, as well as athletic identity and diversity in sport. Rasmussen's main research has centered on Scholar Baller, an academic motivational program that incorporates popular culture to help bridge the gap between education, entertainment and sport. Her most recent article, "Pride Is All You Need," which outlines ways to strengthen a high school athletic program, was published in *Athletic Management.*

Joshua C. Watson is an associate professor of counselor education in the department of counseling and educational psychology at Texas A&M University in Corpus Christi. Watson's research interests include counseling issues surrounding college student-athletes, best practices in counseling assessment, and adolescent wellness. He currently serves as editor of the *Journal of College Counseling* and has published in over 60 professional publications including articles appearing in *the Journal of College Student Development,* the *Journal of College Counseling,* and the *College Student Journal.* Watson also is coauthor of the textbook *Counseling Assessment and Evaluation: Fundamentals of Applied Practice.*

INDEX

Making the Connection, pages 157–160
Copyright © 2015 by Information Age Publishing

CPSIA information can be obtained
at www.ICGtesting.com
Printed in the USA
FSOW04n1650071216
28065FS